Alaska Wilderness Hunter

Alaska Wilderness Hunter
by: Harold Schetzle

*Great Northwest Publishing
and Distributing Company, Inc.
Anchorage, Alaska
1987*

Copyright © 1987 by Harold Schetzle
ALL RIGHTS RESERVED
ISBN 0-937708-12-7
Printed in the United States of America
First Edition 1987
Third Printing 1998

DEDICATION

To all the friends I've shared campfires and siwashed with — and to the ones whose turn is coming.

To my Mom (Daisy Ellen Schetzle, may her beautiful spirit rest in peace) and Dad for imparting a love of wilderness and hunting and helping in my quest to become a guide and outdoor writer.

To Glo, my wife, and hunting partner, for her love, help, encouragement and patience. And daughters, Shannon and Kichana, who reluctantly put up with Dad's annual three months of guiding.

ACKNOWLEDGEMENTS

To Professor Charles J. Keim, Alaskan guide, writer and writing teacher extraordinaire, for his friendship and encouragement to put my adventures on paper and his suggestion to put this collection together.

To Marvin H. Clark, Jr., publisher, for his interest and help in preparing this book.

FOREWORD

Thankfully, Harold Schetzle is one of millions of Americans taught by their fathers to use a firearm properly, then share hunts. As son and father, I can testify that this is a prideful experience, and important to the nation.

I have a somewhat similar, but dual, feeling about Harold. First, there's the sense of pride over this Vietnam Veteran's accomplishments as a widely published writer since he first arrived at the University of Alaska, where I became his professor/friend. Second, while I was serving as a registered big game guide on the Alaska Guide Licensing and Control Board, I watched Harold develop from assistant to highly respected fair chase guide. Later, I could assure him from afar, "You have the know-how; don't worry about your passing the examinations for Master guide."

Today he holds that honorable professional position — hard earned, but auguring well for hunters who increasing seek this highly experienced outdoorsman's expert services. They are a diversity of hunters, from the United States, New Zealand, France, Germany, Norway, and our good friend and neighbor, Canada. And they can "book" to hunt for a diversity of big game with modern firearms, muzzle loaders, archery and camera.

There are many persons, of course, who for a number of reasons cannot actively participate in such Alaskan wilderness hunts with Harold, or swap stories, maybe even a few "tall tales" with him around the campfire. Vicariously, they'll be able to participate by reading this, his first book, ALASKA WILDERNESS HUNTER. When they complete reading, they'll want to call Harold by the same name as do his other warm friends: "Zeke." Read the book, and do it. You're going to get to know this writer/guide better!

Charles J. Keim

CONTENTS

Chapter	I	The Making Of A Wilderness Hunter	15
Chapter	II	Fair Chase	21
Chapter	III	Old Broken Horn	29
Chapter	IV	Too Late To Back Down	53
Chapter	V	World Record For A Week	63
Chapter	VI	Alaska Range Ram	75
Chapter	VII	The Granddaddy Of Zachar Bay	83
Chapter	VIII	Strange Year Of One-Antlered Moose	89
Chapter	IX	Poncho-Bush Country Survivor	91
Chapter	X	Ten Feet To Oblivion	95
Chapter	XI	Black Bears of Prince William Sound	121
Chapter	XII	Double On Deer	129
Chapter	XIII	Siwash Survival	137
Chapter	XIV	King Of The Mountain	143
Chapter	XV	Big Bore For Big Bear	151
Chapter	XVI	Alaska Range Trapline	157
Chapter	XVII	Alder Mania	183
Chapter	XVIII	Battered But Not Beaten	191
Chapter	XIX	Family Trapline In The Alaskan Wilds	199
Chapter	XX	A Guide To Guided Hunts	207

KICHATNA *GUIDE SERVICE*

P.O. Box 670790
Chugiak
Alaska 99567
(907) 696-3256

Harold Schetzle
(Zeke)
Master Guide

**Specializing In:
Rifle, Muzzleloader, Archery
Hunts and Photography Trips**

CHAPTER I

THE MAKING OF A WILDERNESS HUNTER

According to Dad I had the makings of a hunter at an early age. Before I could read I spent hours poring over Outdoor Life magazines and pestered him with questions about the animals. Dad was a hunter himself, more meat than trophy, whose preferred game animal was elk. As a logger in Idaho's Selway Mountains he brought me up on wild game and during my early years I didn't like chicken or beef, preferring pheasant, elk and deer. As a four year old I hand-fed salt to elk and deer while Mom and Dad kept a close eye from the house doorway.

I don't recall much about my earliest hunting escapades but as a six year old I remember my first BB gun. And later on, receiving an admonishment from dad, "Get a bucket of water and if you see any snakes (Diamond back rattler country) leave them alone."

Sure enough I came around a corner and there was a big rattler sidling across the trail. This was my chance. I dropped the bucket, whipped up my BB gun and opened fire. The rattler coiled and became a mite perturbed as I fired salvo after salvo. I lost track of time and the next thing I knew the old man grabbed me and whacked my backside severely. He finished the snake off with a .22 pistol as I watched through my tears. That was my first acquaintance with Robert Rouark's principle of "use enough gun."

In August 1956, Dad and Mom herded the family together and, with another family, headed up the Alcan highway for Alaska. My youngest brother, Brian, was two then and rode in front with Mom and Dad while Randy (four) and I rode beneath a tarp in the pickup bed, the whites of our eyes like ivory billard balls under the Edmonton prairie dust as we convoyed to Alaska.

Dad and his partner, Darrell Gardner, planned to log in Southeast but missed the road and headed toward Anchorage. Our old pickup died just outside of town, near Ship Creek, and we camped there (unknowingly on Fort Richardson army reservation lands) until the military police visited us. Mom was washing diapers in the creek and an aghast MP said, "Lady, you can't do that there, that's the city's water supply."

After that memorable start, we lived in Anchorage for a couple years before moving to Chugiak, 17 miles from Anchorage. It wasn't like elk hunting with horses in Idaho but Dad always got his moose in the fall and I loved the cool, misty mornings and the putt-putt sound of the '52 Willys Jeep as we cruised the backroad and trails. Then he would whisper, "Hand me the rifle," and the pre-64 Winchester .338 would roar and we'd have our meat supply for the winter.

On one occasion we made a wrong turn and started into the Fort Richardson military reservation near Eagle River. As we rounded a corner we looked into the culvert size muzzle of a tank cannon. Needless to say, Dad slammed the Willy's into reverse and got us out of there.

Smiling, he said, "We were a mite outgunned."

My first big game rifle came shortly afterward and was the worst kicking rifle I've ever owned, a Winchester .308. It didn't fit, but at $50 I couldn't expect much. Dad put in half and I earned the other half with a friend as we dug a 20 foot deep well for 50 cents an hour.

Dad later helped me restock the .308 with an American Walnut stock from Herter's and it became a good shooter. The following year I was 14 and accompanied Dad and a friend on a November caribou hunt near Squaw Creek in the Talkeetna Mountains. We jumped several caribou and Dad and his buddy both shot at a distant big one while the others thundered over a snowy ridge to our right. I snapped one shot off just as they disappeared over the crest.

The big one escaped unscathed despite all the shooting and I ended up with my first caribou, a cow, taken with a neck shot at 150 yards.

My fledging hunting career continued with other caribou hunts, some successful, others not. In high school, another hunter destined to be guide, Karl Braendel, and I started running a winter trapline and hunting spring and fall up Eagle River, just 15 miles from Anchorage. Anchorage had half the population it does now and the hunting up Eagle River was made to order for low budget hunters. The seasons were liberal as well as the game available: you could take three mountain goats, a moose, a Dall sheep, three black bear and a brown/grizzly bear (seen infrequently).

Our hunting efforts were unsuccessful half the time but we persevered and improved. Through occasional blunders we accumulated lessons in survival by being caught on a mountain and siwashing, nearly drowning crossing the river, almost sinking in a raft loaded with two goats, battling alders (one of the best techniques for learning to deal with your temper) and backpacking duffel bags loaded with canned food lashed to surplus army pack boards. Our best hunt produced two mountain goats whose horns scored 48 when the Boone & Crockett minimum was 49.

Other trips with friends and brothers provided experiences such as black bear destroying a spike camp and eating all the food, and a scope fogging just before my chance for a large Dall ram.

High school graduation came in May 1966 and prom night was memorable for Karl and I. That night we crosscountry skiied our trapline trail and returned with two blanket and one medium beaver. I guess that should have told us that we were likely to become guides, but our high school yearbook said differently.

Karl's interests were in animal farming while I intended to become a geologist. Due to financial and draft considerations though, I enlisted in the Navy, and after boot camp went to radar school.

A steel ship (U.S.S. Seminole - AKA-104) wasn't an ideal place for an outdoor oriented teenager and it required a serious effort in adapting. The lessons of close range living would later serve me well though.

My buddy, Karl, had done so much shooting in his early years that the service wouldn't take him because of hearing loss; it was their loss since he is one of the finest shots I have seen. Karl became an assistant guide shortly afterward.

The Phillipines and Vietnam nearly made a baked Alaskan out of me, but the desire for hunting didn't die. Karl and I wrote occasionally and set up a brown bear hunt on Kodiak Island when my leave came up. Our first hunt at Hidden Basin in May 1968 was unsuccessful, but we were fortunate to escape with our lives when a large avalanche nearly caught us as we stalked a bear sleeping on a steep snowslide. If we had been 50 yards closer and fired a shot the avalanche would have caught us.

In May 1969 I was back home on leave and much to my mother's consternation went hunting again, returning to Kodiak for brown bear with Karl. We were more fortunate then and with Karl's help, I took a tough 8 1/2 foot bear in Zachar Bay with a Winchester .338 I had picked up in Japan in 1968. At the age of 20 I had taken my first brown bear.

My tour of service with Navy ended in August of 1970 when I was accepted by the University of Alaska in Fairbanks. It wasn't easy but I squeezed in a sheep hunt with my Dad and younger brother before school started. As usual it was another adventure.

Hugging the cliffs along a long gravel slide, we climbed after a ram we had seen on a rock outcrop where two narrow ravines joined to form the big one we were on. We had previously decided Dad would get the first shot and when we got close I advised him to get ready.

Stepping out, Dad raised his Winchester .338 and looked through the scope. Suddenly he fired, the shot startling us.

A muffled curse and he fired again. I stepped out and glimpsed a golden horned white shape disappearing 100 yards above us. Swinging the .338 I touched off a shot and the ram dropped out of sight. Brian took off like a shot while Dad and I climbed at a more leisurely pace.

"What happened?" I asked.

"Take a look," he said, still cursing.

I raised the scope to my eye and looked through an empty tube. The crosshairs had collapsed. It was Dad's first and last sheep hunt, he didn't think he could survive another one like that.

The 3/4 curl ram was lying six feet from the edge of a sheer drop of several hundred feet. Lady Luck must have had a hand in that, plus skeet shooting practice in the Navy, for the quick running shot.

Never a mathematician, calculus (and the prospect of two semesters of differential equations afterward) finished me off in the second year of college. I gained an interest in writing though, and it was encouraged by a magazine article writing course taught by Professor Charles Keim (well known author of "Alaska Game Trails with a Master Guide") and further encouraged by Sam Fadala, friend and teacher's assistant (now a renowned blackpowder expert and author of ten books on shooting and hunting).

My buddy Karl contacted me that summer and mentioned that he had recommended me to a guide who was short handed for the coming fall. From there it was all down hill or up, depending on how you look at it.

"You'll never make anything of yourself guiding," Dad said more than once. "I've known a few of them and they don't have a pot to pee in."

I suppose that's mostly true, I don't know any rich guides. But they have a wealth of experience and good health.

I worked as an assistant guide for Dennis Harms of Chugiak from '72-75', hunting Kodiak, the Wrangell's during the big sheep years, B.C. (before Carter), Talkeetna's, and the big moose years on the Alaska Peninsula. In July 1975 I received my registered license, AA-0377, in 1987 my Master Guide license, and along with the support and assistance of Mom & Dad, and clients throughout the U.S. and other countries, and family, two daughters, Shannon and Kichana, and working wife, Gloria Fawcett Schetzle, have been and continue to operate Kichatna Guide Service out of Chugiak, Alaska.

CHAPTER II

FAIR CHASE

You've hoarded your nickels and dimes for years and finally made it to Alaska, the great land of towering, snow-capped mountains, crevassed glaciers, giant moose, Kodiak bear, nomadic caribou, and 40-inch Dall sheep. Your childhood dream is materializing.

Your bearded guide meets you in Anchorage, and a few hours later you're in the wilderness. You get settled in at camp and check your rifle at a makeshift range. The guide asks if you want to look over the country before supper. You jump at the chance. "Might as well bring along your rifle," he adds. "In case we need it for survival purposes."

Buzzing along in the Supercub through the low clouds, your guide, who is also your pilot, circles a respectable bull moose in the 55-inch class. You're amazed at the animal's size. "Whitetails sure don't look like that," you gasp.

Your guide continues searching the swamps and lakes. There he is, a monster of a moose, a 65 to 70-inch spread. You lean forward and half yell. "That's the kind I want!"

"Let's take a closer look," the guide says. He makes a couple of circles, scanning the sky for other aircraft. The bull is near a lake, and the guide puts the floatplane down smoothly and taxis as close to the moose as he can. "Come on, let's see how big he really is," he says.

You instinctively grab your rifle and follow him into the brush. A few minutes elapse, then you see antler tips gleaming above the alders. The bull moves off, but you have time for a quick shot when he steps into a small clearing. You get a sudden mental flash — Alaska's game regulations forbid the taking of big game the same day you are airborne.

What would you do?

The guide knows it's illegal, but it's a risk he's willing to take. Alaska's Fish & Game protection agents have a tremendous land mass to keep under surveillance with limited personnel and resources, so the guide is gambling that he won't get caught. He knows his clients aren't interested in tales of good hunts where the big one got away; they want to hear about his 100 percent success ratio. And many could care less how he maintains it.

"Take him," the guide whispers.

You jerk the Winchester .338 to your shoulder, center the crosshairs of the Leupold 4X in the dark crease behind the bull's shoulder, and apply pressure to the trigger. In a millisecond, the giant moose will be yours, and you can hear the boys back home envying you already.

Your brain slowly takes over, and you lower your rifle and say, "I can't."

"What the hell. What do you mean you can't?" the guide hisses.

"It's a matter of ethics," you reply as the moose fades out of sight.

Ethics, according to the college edition of the New Webster's Dictionary, "is the rules of conduct recognized in respect to a particular class of human actions: as in medical ethics: moral principles, as of an individual."

There are unethical guides like the fictional one mentioned, but they are slowly being weeded out of the ranks of Alaska's professional guides. Guides are people (despite some claims to the contrary) with the foibles common to all humans. Occasionally, the pursuit of money due to circumstance overshadows personal moral codes.

But it takes both a hunter and a guide in collaboration to get into a situation like the aforementioned one. Both hunter and guide should check values with one another, each helping the other to overcome a temporary lapse in moral judgment.

In 1975, I guided a hunter from New York on a moose hunt. He seemed like a nice guy, a little high strung from work pressures but otherwise fine. We hunted a few days without seeing any big bulls, and one afternoon we shortened our hunting day to meet a Supercub bringing in supplies.

"Hey, did you guys see that big bull just over the ridge?" the pilot asked.

The hunter and I looked at each other in surprise. We had traveled that area earlier without seeing anything.

The pilot pointed over the ridge and said. "He's only 400 yards away."

"Let's go, what are we waiting for?" the hunter asked.

"You can't use an airplane to spot game," I said.

"I didn't. He did," the hunter replied.

"Yes, but we wouldn't have known the bull was there without the plane," I said.

The pilot unloaded and roared off. "Come on, let's get the bull," the hunter pleaded.

"We can't," I said.

The hunter's face reddened, and he didn't speak to me the rest of the day. As we headed back to the cabin that evening, he finally said, "I guess you were right." We tentatively began discussing ethics and hunting. I had recently read "Meditations on Hunting," by Spanish philosopher Jose Ortega Y Gasset, and recommended it to him.

On hunting ethics, Mr. Gasset wrote: "The hunter who accepts the sporting code of ethics keeps his commandments in the greatest solitude, with no witnesses or audience other than the sharp peaks of the mountains."

My hunter shot his moose later in the hunt. Since then we have shared many campfires and hunts and have built a lasting friendship.

This man saw the light, but we've all heard of those who haven't. One of the most blatant cases in the past occurred when both the editor and the publisher of a well-known hunting magazine were arrested and convicted of violating Alaska game laws. They put out a good magazine, and I thought they were fair chase oriented. The hunters were on a brown/grizzly bear hunt with handguns. The hunters took a stand while their pilot herded bear to them. It would have been interesting to see the article they would have written about that hunt.

Hunting ethics can vary in degree of interpretation among individuals. A few years back, a 20-year-old assistant guide and I were laid back in a log cabin discussing hunting. Our guiding season had ended, but grizzly season was open, and the assistant guide wanted one badly.

"I wish an old griz would walk by right now," he said, gazing out the window. "I'd let him have it."

"You wouldn't appreciate it." I said.

"What do you mean?" he asked.

"There wouldn't be anything to it," I said. "You wouldn't have hunted or worked for it. There wouldn't be any meaning and very little memory; you might as well have bought it. Sure, there would be a little rush of excitement, but that would soon disappear."

"Now if you had your pack on and were heading out hunting, it would be different," I continued. "Say you saw the bear in some brush 100 yards from the cabin, stalked it, and then shot it. The bear would have had a fair chance, more so than being ambushed from the cabin door. Your mental outlook would have been different; you would have been hunting."

"I don't see any difference," he replied.

Hopefully he'll realize the ethics of hunting one of these days. Then maybe he will see the difference.

Other violations of ethics are more visible. Several years ago, I guided a hunter after moose and grizzly in the Alaska Range. The day after he arrived by bush plane, we took a boat upriver to some good moose country. It was raining, and we eased along the edges of a swamp in search of a bull.

After four hours of hunting, the hunter wanted to turn back, but I talked him into climbing a low ridge to check a grassy clearing I had found while trapping in the area the preceding winter. As we topped the ridge, we spotted a bull digging a rut pit not 35 yards away. It took three shots from the hunter's .358 to bring him down.

"You've got a good bull," I happily said, slapping the hunter on the back.

We walked up to the 62½-inch bull, and as I stood admiring him the hunter grunted, "Will he make the Boone and Crockett book?"

I studied the antlers and said, "No, I don't think so, but he'll be close."

The hunter uttered a four-letter word and kicked the moose in the neck. I looked at him incredulously. One of the nicest moose I'd ever seen, and this guy didn't even want it. He hadn't mentioned anything about the Boone and Crockett record book before we started hunting.

I'm slow to get riled (a good attribute to have as a guide), but I came close to unloading on the hunter right then and there. I finished caping and field-dressing the moose without speaking to him. The Boone and Crockett book requires 224 points for Alaska-Yukon moose — his bull scored 218.

Hunting ethics also involves respect for the animals you hunt.

When it was legal to shoot the same day as airborne, a guide I was working for let an older hunter from Wisconsin shoot a caribou from the float of his plane. "It's like shooting a cow in your backyard," I told the hunter's son.

The son nodded in assent but didn't say much.

Is it always necessary to get a trophy when you hunt, regardless of the mental consequences? I can't see how a person feels quite right or explains how they got the animal to family and friends when they take game illegally. Think back on your hunts. Is the largest trophy you've taken the most vivid memory? Or is it the one where you froze your butt off in a rainstorm or blizzard, and on the last day of your hunt, after having passed up a few smaller animals, made a perfect stalk and shot an average animal?

I shot my best Sitka blacktail deer on Kodiak Island. The buck walked out of a ravine about 50 yards away - an easy shot. But the buck that means the most to me is a five-point buck that I jumped about 40 yards away and couldn't get a shot at. As he bounded off, I spotted a small opening 150 yards ahead of him, put my crosshairs at shoulder height, and waited. When he entered the clearing, I squeezed off the shot. I took me five minutes to find him stone dead in the grass.

The Boone and Crockett record book isn't that important to me. However, to many sportsmen it's the true measure of a trophy. If it makes the "book," it's something to brag about. I know of two trophies in the book that are examples of book entries rather than hunting experiences; a caribou taken by landing a plane next to a herd and shooting the bull, and a Mountain goat shot by a hunter from a snow machine.

To me, the book is primarily a guide of how large a species may get. If an animal qualifies, that's frosting on the cake. The Boone and Crockett Club strongly advocates fair chase and hunting ethics, but it's difficult to keep out those hunters who would do anything to get their name in the book.

Hunting the same day you are airborne is a serious violation of Alaska's game laws. Nonresidents should be aware of this law and not be led into an unethical and unlawful position where they could face a fine, imprisonment, or confiscation of their firearms or trophies. I would enjoin all nonresident hunters coming to Alaska or any other state to read the hunting regulations and adhere to them closely.

After all, it's a matter of ethics.

CHAPTER III

OLD BROKEN HORN

"Careful, don't skyline yourself," my hunting partner, Doug McRae, cautioned. "We'd better stick close to the cliff face."

We slowly climbed the last few yards of a grass-covered ridge in eastern Alaska's rugged Wrangell Mountains, our mouths wind-dried and hearts thumping wildly. Miles of glacial moraine and ice stretched through the valley below us.

The Wrangells remain much as they were during the last Pleistocene glaciation stage, some 11,000 years ago, which covered parts of Alaska, Canada, and the continental United States. Snow and ice-capped peaks are split in places by massive glaciers. Valleys gouged by roaring streams are numerous, and vary from vertical rock to lush, grass-blanketed slopes. Much of this vast area is traveled by golden-horned Dall sheep, shaggy Mountain goats, and an occasional wandering grizzly.

The particular ram that we were hunting had been stalked before. Doug had guided Dick Martin, a non-resident hunter, in quest of a broken horn ram without knowing how large it really was; in fading light he had estimated the ram's good horn at 41 inches. Now the hunter had gone home, and Doug and I were taking up the trail.

I enjoy hunting Alaska's white sheep and Mountain goats more than any other of its big-game species. It stems from the rugged but beautiful terrain and the continual suspense involved in stalking the quarry. Dall sheep are generally easy to spot, but reaching them and getting back down often isn't.

Anticipation prodded us awake at 3:30 in the morning, and after a candlelight oatmeal breakfast, we were on our way by 4 a.m.

Scattered clouds drifted by the moon's face as we fumbled our way along an alder-lined trail enroute to the ice and moraine-filled valley where Doug had last seen Old Broken Horn. Soon we walked in the shadows of jagged mountains, silhouetted like shark's teeth against the coming dawn.

We wanted to approach the ram's territory before daylight, and this forced us to travel a more circuitous route through the rock piles to escape detection. The morning chill foretold the approaching end of sheep season and the beginning of winter; snow already covered the upper third of the mountains. This assisted us by pushing the sheep down from the crags and out of the high-elevation tributary valleys.

We traveled in the depressions between moraine hills until Doug knew we were in the big ram's locality. Shortly before 7 o'clock we scrambled to the top of a prominent hill to look around. Doug set up his spotting scope while I glassed the valley walls with my 7x35 binoculars. A gray curtain of overcast had moved in since we started, carrying with it a mixture of fog and low clouds that suggested rain or snow.

Looking down valley, we spotted four rams on a rocky outcrop, but the largest was only a light-horned full curl. Minutes later Doug spied a white dot across the valley and studied it intently.

"It's just a big Mountain goat," he grunted.

A few seconds later he laughed and said, "Take a look at

this, he's stuck on the edge of a cliff."

I didn't quite believe it, but looked through his spotting scope anyway. Sure enough, that bewildered billy goat was in a place he couldn't go down or around. He stood there for a couple of minutes, twisting his bearded head back and forth, searching for a way out, but finally had to back up.

We moved up the glacier and crawled to the top of a higher rock pile. It didn't take Doug long to find another white speck across the valley.

"He's just a full curl," sighed Doug.

"Wait a minute," I cautioned. "Look a little below that ram and to his right."

Doug moved the spotting scope slightly.

"I think it's Old Broken Horn!" he said. "He's lying down facing away from us, but his bases are really heavy."

Suddenly the big ram stood up.

"Take a look at this," Doug gasped.

I eased behind the spotting scope and gazed at a sight guaranteed to nearly paralyze any sheep hunter. The huge ram's broken horn was visible.

After another quick glance I surrendered the scope to Doug.

"Look, now you can see his good horn, it must be between forty-four and forty-six inches!"

The two rams hadn't spotted us yet, but the upper one unexpectedly moved across a rock slide and disappeared behind a ridge while Old Broken Horn slowly began grazing up the valley.

We studied the mountain and searched for a route that would place us in shooting range of the big ram. The obvious strategy would be to get above him, since sheep and goats tend to be less watchful from this direction. While discussing different approaches we spotted the Mountain goat again. This time he was climbing directly toward the rams.

Doug lashed his spotting scope to his packboard and we

began angling across the glacier. A small stream bisected it, leaving steep, glassy ice faces that we had to slide down. One slip here could have meant a broken ankle. Getting out was like climbing up a descending escalator.

Reaching the base of the mountain we clawed our way up a steep gravel slide. Doug carried his rifle, 100 feet of 3/8-inch nylon rope, spotting scope and tripod, all tied on his packboard. My packsack contained camera gear, binoculars, two hunting knives, spare eyeglasses, first aid kit, a Space Blanket, meat bags, and a Knapp meat saw.

Our stalk was progressing well until light rain began to fall and the rocks became slippery. We tried to keep on grassy areas, but were often forced to cross boulder-strewn slides as we angled up the mountain.

We stopped to rest and I dried my glasses while we discussed whether to circle around below the rams or continue angling up despite the Mountain goat's presence.

"I bet that goat is lying right about where we want to shoot from," Doug whispered. "Sure hope he doesn't scare the sheep."

Three hundred yards above, light snow extended like fingers into some rocky ravines. We headed for the grassy ridge behind which the smaller ram had disappeared. The Mountain goat had been headed for this same ridge.

Following a faintly etched sheep trail around the base of a sheer cliff, we started up the last steep stretch to the ridge top, which butted against a rock outcrop. Twenty yards from the top Doug eased around the side and spotted the big billy lying down with his head pointed up-valley.

Doug slid back down and we continued along just below the spine of the ridge.

We moved slowly for the last few steps in order to catch our breath. A slight breeze carried our scent up the mountain.

Doug carefully poked his head over the ridge top and quickly dropped back below the crest.

Zeke with near record book Mountain goat taken up Eagle River in August 1965. This billy was dropped with one shot from a re-stocked Husquarvna .30-06 and the horns scored 48 when Boone & Crockett minimum was 49. Photo by Karl Braendel.

Author with a 63½ inch bull moose rack taken in the Shotgun Hills area of southwestern Alaska. Bull was called in by Zeke and dropped with one shot at 300 yards by Joe Orr of Shawnee Mission, Kansas, in the fall of 1984. Photo by Joe Orr.

A 7½ inch to 8 inch billy that we passed up (John Babler and I) on his Mountain goat hunt in the Wrangell Mountains. Ram Glacier lies in the valley bottom.

Author's wife, Gloria (Fawcett) Schetzle with a fine 38 inch Dall sheep taken near the South Fork of the Kuskokwim River in the Alaska Range. The big ram was taken with one shot from a Remington .270 at 200 yards.

Author searches for route up a rock face while stalking a Dall sheep with John Babler, Jr. of White Bear, Minnesota, in the Wrangell Mountains near Chitina Glacier. Photo by John Babler.

John Babler Jr. with excellent Mountain goat taken up Ram Glacier in the Wrangell Mountains. This nanny's horns were 9¾ inches long and goat was taken with .300 Weatherby.

Author with heavily broomed, old ram taken by John Babler Jr. of White Bear, Minnesota with a .300 Weatherby in 1972 in the Wrangell Mountains near Chitina Glacier. Photo by John Babler.

Zeke, on left, and Doug McRae, Sr. of Seward, Alaska with the big ram that scored 171 3/8 and ranks 191 in the 1981 Boone & Crockett record book. Rams like this usually come once in a lifetime but Doug has two other rams in the 40 inch class.

Gloria (Glo) Fawcett Schetzle, author's wife and life long Alaskan with her eight foot Kodiak brown bear taken near Uganik Lake, Kodiak Island in 1980. An old sow, the bear was shot at 50 feet with a .270 Winchester. Bear rolled down a creek gully and was finished with author's .338 Winchester as she staggered up bank. First shot had been right behind the shoulder. Glo's bear has the white claws indicative of an old bear.

Doug McRae of Seward, Alaska with a beautiful long haired Mountain goat taken near Seward in October 1972 with a 7mm magnum. This nice billy went 9½ inches. On the same trip the author took a nanny that measured 9¼ inches.

Don Fraser of Dearborn Heights, Michigan, cautiously approaches a fine caribou he shot in southwest Alaska, Shotgun Hills on a September 1984 hunt.

Zeke capes 61½ inch moose taken by Jack Wolfner of St. Louis, Missouri near the King Salmon River, Alaska Peninsula in 1973. Once a moose is down, several hours of work are necessary to cape, butcher and pack meat out.

Zeke on his favorite horse, Poncho, leads pack horse, Big Boy, on return to camp with Ron Kolpin's caribou taken in September 1974 in the Alaska Range. Keeping your feet out, or just the tips of your boots in the stirrups, is wise when crossing rivers in the event your horse rolls. Photo by Ron Kolpin.

Ornery one-antlered bull that approached our horses and seemed to be overly interested in two of our mares, even had the geldings worried. The bull had apparently come out on the losing end of a sparring match during the September rut.

Ron Kolpin of Berlin, Wisconsin with his "world record for a week," bull that he took in the Alaska Range Mountains in September 1974. The 62 inch bull is listed as number five in the 1981 Pope & Young record book.

Norwegian Oystein Herstad on right and Zeke with congratulatory handshake after stalking within 12 yards and taking this 68½ inch moose. Bull was dropped with one shot from a custom .338 Sako in September 1981 in the Alaska Range Mountains and narrowly missed the Boone & Crockett record book.

Zeke calls moose while New Zealander, Keith Purdon, waits for one to show. The art of moose calling is growing in Alaska, due in part to the establishment of the International Moose Federation and their promotion of an annual moose calling contest.

New Zealander, Keith Purdon, lowers his .308 Remington after shooting a nice bull behind shoulder; blown hair is visible where bullet struck. Bull took two more shots to Keith's amazement and required another finishing shot.

Keith Purdon of Auckland, New Zealand, with his heavy horned bull moose with a spread of 57¼ inches (note extra point coming off beam by brow tines) taken in September 1983.

Don Fraser of Dearborn Heights, Michigan, with a beautiful bull caribou taken in the Shotgun Hills, southwest Alaska, during September 1984 hunt.

Ron Arch of Hopatcong, New Jersey, with a large black bear taken in the Alaska Range Mountains that squared 6'3" and whose skull made Pope & Young (bowhunter's record book) with a score of 18 3/16. Using a Stemmler bow, Ron arrowed the bear with a perfect shot behind the shoulder but the bear went into some dense willows.

Bill Sanders of Washington, Pennsylvania, with a fair bull called in by Zeke and taken with one shot from Bill's .60 side by side double barrel muzzleloader at 100 yards with a neck shot. Bull taken September 6, 1980.

"I just saw one or maybe two sheep; they're looking up this way; I may have to shoot in a hurry!" he gasped.

Doug shuffled along on his elbows and knees, pushing his coat and 7mm magnum rifle through the wet grass into a slight depression on the ridge. I followed close behind and peeked over the depression's edge to check on the Mountain goat that threatened to spoil our stalk. The big billy should have been lying peacefully some 50 yards below us.

"He's standing and looking here!"

We were only about 80 yards from Old Broken Horn and the other, smaller Dall ram. Both were seconds from spooking as they warily watched the shaggy goat and looked up toward our vantage point.

Doug put his crosshairs on the big ram's shoulder.

"I can't shoot. His broken horn is in the way."

I raised up slightly and snapped a picture of the two rams.

Suddenly Doug exclaimed, "I'm gonna shoot, I'm gonna shoot!"

With the sharp crack of the 7mm the two rams whirled around and began running. Doug fired again and again only to watch them veer around a rock outcrop and disappear into a ravine. He jumped up and waited for the sheep to reappear... but they didn't.

We looked on both sides of the ridge for the old billy but he had wisely made himself scarce.

"I must have had a case of buck fever, that's the only way I could miss like that, unless my sights are off," Doug moaned as he kicked grass.

"I even had a perfect rest," he agonized.

With our hearts in our boots we turned and looked back to where the sheep had vanished. Our jaws nearly came unhinged when the two rams popped into view 175 yards away, climbing out of the ravine.

Doug instantly flopped down in the grass and fired. Old Broken Horn was walking slowly up the side of the ravine when a 175-grain bullet smashed him between the front shoulders.

I watched through my 200mm lens as the big ram started rolling, picked up speed, somersaulted 20 feet in the air off an outcrop, bounced a couple of times, and disappeared.

We waited for our hearts to resume a near-regular beat, and started down after the ram.

Reaching the cliff where he had fallen off we quickly spotted him on a talus slide. I pulled the binoculars out of my pack and looked at the ram.

"I think one horn is missing," I said slowly.

Doug untied his spotting scope and confirmed my statement.

Five or six hundred feet of nearly sheer cliff convinced us of the impossibility of descending here. So we followed the cliff's edge, searching for an alternate route down, rather than retracing our tracks to the glacier and then having to climb a chute to reach the ram.

Climbing up, we soon discovered a narrow rock chute that led to a gravel valley on the same level as the ram.

Doug rolled a shotput-sized rock into the chute and we followed its progress with interest. Near the bottom it bounced out into space, disappeared, and then reappeared, rolling to a stop on a fanlike slide in the valley.

Halfway down we used Doug's dangle rope for safety's sake, being careful not to dislodge any rock slabs from the heavily fractured walls. A simultaneous sigh of relief escaped us when we reached the bottom.

We followed the cliff's base before coming out in the main valley. Crossing the head of a treacherous-looking slide, we finally reached Doug's ram.

We started searching the slide for the missing horn, hoping that it hadn't lodged in the inaccessible rocks. Nearly five minutes went by before Doug found it lying in some boulders.

Pausing awhile, we admired the broomed-off horn and then walked down to the ram. Doug's final shot had made the only bullet hole we found. Neither of us had a tape measure, so I removed my belt and we came up with 44 inches for the good horn and 35 for the broken one.

Fog was rolling in as I hastily snapped some pictures. Completing that, we worked on the ram and loaded our packs. Another chute provided our only route down. This one had concrete-hard mud walls and loose gravel underfoot that made our progress a little faster than desired at times.

The heavy packs with meat, horns, and cape, made it difficult to maintain our balance. Rounding a projecting part of the wall I leaped to the other side, but the pack off-balanced me and I teetered on the verge of tumbling down the chute. I plastered myself against the wall and breathlessly regained my footing.

Near the bottom of the chute we tied the ends of our dangle rope together so it could be retrieved, and hooked one end around a partially exposed rock to serve as a balancing aid for the remainder of the descent.

Reaching the glacier, we rested for ten minutes before heading to camp. On our way down-valley we caught the four sheep we spotted that morning, much lower than usual. From their startled reactions they apparently weren't expecting us to return.

We stumbled into spike camp just before darkness, two exhausted but happy hunters.

In December 1972, Doug had Old Broken Horn officially measured for the Boone and Crockett Record book. The ram's right horn was 36 3/8 inches, his left stretched the tape to an even 44 inches. The left horn measured 14 5/8 inches in circumference; the right one was 14 3/4 inches. The total score was 171 3/8 points. We compared it to the 1971 record book entries and it ranked in a tie for 160th place. If the right horn hadn't been broken, it may have had eight points more, which would have placed it in the top twenty.

In the course of the hunt, we crossed a boulder-strewn slide on which rested the weathered skull of a sheep. A splintered brown horn protruded from the skull, and it must have measured between 40 and 42 inches. It struck me that here died a fine trophy animal, killed by wolves or weather or slow starvation; a great animal, perished anonymously.

But Old Broken Horn will occupy an honored place on Doug's wall. His end, after a long life, was quick. And most important, he will be admired and remembered.

(Reprinted with permission from Field & Stream magazine)

CHAPTER IV

TOO LATE TO BACK DOWN!

We couldn't wage warfare against the horde of Alaskan mosquitos that swarmed us as we suffered quietly in thigh-high grass and watched a tangled stretch of alders below. Forty yards into the maze we could discern the dark mass of a feeding Kodiak brown bear.

As we intently watched the bear, it surprisingly began advancing, it's movement signaled by swaying alder tops.

My pulse quickened as I realized how dangerous a situation we had stumbled into. Our backs were against a wall of alders and our field of shooting severely limited. The narrow clearing we were in stretched laterally along the mountain for a short distance but it was too late to move away.

The spring of 1973 began no differently than many others I've spent on Kodiak Island. For three days the wind-lashed rain beat an intermittent tattoo on the tiny cabin's tin roof. Dennis Harms, registered guide and outfitter, and our next hunter, G. Schuster, a 54 year old Minnesota machinery manufacturer, were two days late. An assistant guide at the time, I was impatiently waiting out the storm, observing grounded seagulls and long necked cormorants perched on the derelict pilings of an old cannery.

Late in the afternoon of May 7th, G.S. chugged in via fisherman's dory after transferring from a Widgeon (a twin engined amphibious plane). Dennis was scheduled in on the eighth, weather permitting.

G.S. and I spent the evening swapping hunting stories and the conversation seldom strayed from Kodiak.

World renown for it's giant bear, Ursus arctos middendorfi, Kodiak Island is the largest island (103 miles long and 53 miles wide) in the Gulf of Alaska. The city of Kodiak, with a population of 5,000, lies on the northeastern tip of the mountainous island. The center of a large fishing industry, Kodiak is also the jumping off point for the islands's guided brown bear hunting industry.

Kodiak Island's bear population is roughly estimated at 3000 bears and the majority of the bears are located on the federally controlled Kodiak Wildlife Refuge. A large southwest area, the refuge contains approximately 2,840 square miles of unbelievable bear country.

The spring bear season on the refuge usually extends from March first to May 15 with the average bear harvest limited to about 140-190 bears annually, including fall.

Nearly hoarse from talking bear, G.S. and I crawled into our sleeping bags for the night, noticing that the rain and wind had tapered off.

When dawn abruptly slipped around, I crow-hopped across the cold floor planks and turned our kerosene stove up. Shortly afterward the pungent smell of coffee and frying bacon mingled, pulling G.S. out of his sleeping bag.

With breakfast out of the way, we dragged a green, 16 foot skiff down the seaweed slickened, gravel beach to salt water. At two-thirds throttle the 9 h.p. Evinrude pushed us quickly to the mouth of a nearby canyon valley. As we pulled the skiff above the debris-marked, high tide line, we saw Dennis circle and land his Supercub near the cabin.

Heading up the canyon valley we approached a grass fringed stream and startled a trotting red fox along an adjacent deer trail. It slapped the brakes on though when our scent eddied to it and disappeared in the blink of an eye. Suddenly, another flash of movement occured.

"What's that?" G.S. snapped, as the flash of brown disappeared.

"Sitka blacktail," I replied, remembering my identical reaction the first time I saw a similar flash of brown on my first Kodiak hunt in 1968.

Introduced to Kodiak in 1924, the blacktails have done well and provide excellent fall hunting, with a five deer limit over most of the island. And just recently the Boone & Crockett record book has accepted these deer as a distinct species for record keeping.

We continued toward the back of Phantom Bear Valley. This uniquely named valley isn't found on any Kodiak maps but derived it's name from the sightings of a long legged, blond bear that a fellow guide and I often spotted between 10 a.m. and noon. The bear stayed close to nasty alder patches and never appeared for more than five to fifteen minutes a day.

I pointed out the circular-shaped clearing where I had last seen the Phantom a week earlier and we glassed the surrounding area. Twenty minutes later we continued hiking over the grass and cottonwood tree covered valley bottom, stopping to glass the brown mountain slopes every 15 minutes or so.

During the spring, Kodiak brown bear can generally be spotted foraging or traveling during the mornings or afternoon-early evening, especially on sunny, windless days. Their preferred foods this time of year are emerging grass shoots and Boschniakia rossica, commonly known as Broomrape, a parasitic plant that acts on alder roots.

The bears tend to bed down around noon for an hour or two and seem to be most active in late afternoon.

It was nearly 2 p.m. when G.S. and I reached a vantage point where we could glass the mile distant, rugged foothills in the rear of the valley.

Sitting on my backpack, I began combing the lower terrain with my 7X35 Bushnell binoculars in a careful side to side squashed "S" pattern.

Half an hour later, I blurted, "There's a bear."

"Where, where?" G.S. asked.

After getting him on the bear I dug out my spotting scope and studied the bear. It was unusually colored black over the front and rear quarters, with a light brown area in between and I checked for rubbed spots. These are often noticeable but I couldn't locate any on the side we could see.

"What do you think?" G.S. asked.

"Looks like it might go nine feet," I said, watching the bear as it ambled aimlessly along the predominantly alder covered, lower mountain slopes.

"But I'm afraid there isn't much of a chance for a stalk," I continued. "Once we headed that way we'd lose sight of the bear and wouldn't have any idea where it went."

G.S. nodded in assent and began glassing for a new bear.

I kept checking the nine-footer's progress but the minutes slipped by without any change and we reluctantly headed for camp.

The return was uneventful and we ate supper and planned the next days' hunt with Dennis.

The next morning, Dennis decided to hunt with us. The weather had improved considerably, seagulls frolicked and two eagles were silhouetted against an azure hole in the scattered cloud cover.

With Dennis at the helm, we cruised along beach hunting and glassing until 10 a.m., then put in at the mouth of Phantom Bear Valley. After unloading some gear I leaned against a wave-eroded rock mass and glassed some of the slopes at the valley entrance.

"See anything?" G.S. hopefully inquired.

"There is a suspicious looking black spot on the left side of the valley," I replied and pointed. "Just above the brush line."

"Just a rock," G.S. declared shortly after checking it with Dennis' 10X binoculars. "It's square on the sides like a statue."

After a look up-valley he swung back to the spot and spoke before I could say anything.

"It just walked off!" he gasped.

Dennis and I decided it was about an eight footer and watched as it plunged through the snow and descended to the brush line and disappeared. G.S. wanted a nine footer anyway.

Hunting along the way we returned to our vantage point of the previous day and, using a space blanket for shelter, ate lunch while waiting out a heavy rain shower. After eating, Dennis took off through the dripping brush to check for bear sign on the north slopes while G.S. and I continued to glass the southern exposures.

Later I spotted a dark bear directly across from our lookout point. Peering through the 40X eyepiece of my spotting scope I estimated the bear would square eight and a half feet (measurement obtained by measuring a bear hide from nose to tail and from front paw to front paw, then adding the two values and dividing by two). At first I thought it might be the bear we had sighted earlier that morning, but then I picked up that bear down valley below some rock ledges.

Dennis joined us about three o'clock and we decided to take a closer look at the bear across from us.

Crossing the valley floor we moved to another hill and endeavored to keep track of the bear, but it began wandering up valley. Shortly afterward we lost it in a wide, alder choked ravine.

Disappointed, we emptied the debris that had fallen in our hipboots and sat down to continue glassing.

"There's another one," Dennis said excitedly.

This bear was about 100 yards from the edge of a large ravine draining a snow patched pass in the mountains. From what I could tell, the bear looked like the same one G.S. and I had seen the day before. We were surprised when it stopped digging at the base of some alders, padded out into a clearing, and laid down on a hummock.

It was 4:30, with four and a half hours of light remaining, and we decided to try for the bear. Dennis carried his open sighted Winchester .375, G.S. his 2X scope sighted Winchester .375 and I trailed behind with my Winchester .338 slung over my shoulder. A 4X scope was mounted on my Pachmayr Lo-Swing top mount and offered me open sights, a feature I would soon appreciate.

Reaching the base of the mountain, we climbed a narrow deer trail, hunched over and crawling half the time. The trail died out and we wove through dense alders along a small stream surrounded by mossy swamp. We followed the creek up mountain until it flowed through a rock walled ravine.

Stopped there, we carefully walked along the ravine's edge and veered away to cross a grassy clearing. The moisture laden ocean breeze was blowing from the bear to us and seemed constant, a plus for our stalk since the bear's nose is it's primary danger warning.

We fought through several frustrating alder patches, like fleas crossing a porcupines' tail, and continued across a dip between two ridges. Near the crest of the upper ridge, Dennis abruptly motioned us to halt.

"Can you see anything?" G.S. whispered.

I shook my head, and we crept forward in response to Dennis' hand signal. As we joined him, he pointed at a dark blob in the alders to our right and slightly down-mountain. It was a different bear than the one we were stalking.

Dennis moved uphill slightly so he could see better. But when he moved, the bear snapped it's head up and looked our way.

G.S. started to join Dennis and I hissed, "Move real slow."

He reached Dennis and I joined them.

Dennis was watching the bear closely and tensely whispered, "We'd better retreat a little."

In a line abreast we slowly stepped backwards a few step.

"He's coming!" Dennis said, a bit incredulously.

"How big is it?" G.S. asked.

"It's a good bear! Shoot! Shoot!" Dennis snapped.

The bear was weaving rapidly through the three and four inch diameter alders. When the brush thinned 50 feet from us the bear was in a full and final charge. The huge head was held low covering the massive chest, it's small, piercing black eyes locked on us, and the jaws closed in silent attack.

My camera dangled from my neck and I had my Winchester in a death grip. I wanted a picture but the bear was so close I quickly flipped my scope to one side.

Standing to G.S.'s right, I planted the bead of my front sight slightly below the bear's black nostrils.

G.S. and Dennis fired nearly simultaneously but I held my fire. As their shots echoed through the valley, the bear crumpled and rolled back into the alders.

It had actually been 50 feet away (later measured by camera) when the two shots were fired.

Rifles at the ready, we edged downhill a short distance until we could see the brown bear more clearly. Sprawled on it's back, the bear breathed a raspy sound, convulsed and moved a front paw.

"Better shoot it again," Dennis advised.

G.S. fired a 300 grain slug into the bear's chest that finished it.

"I see what they mean when they say their head looks like a keg-o-nails," G.S. said in awe as he struggled to lift the shaggy head.

Dennis and I skinned the boar and he seemed to have been in good health, no old wounds and teeth in fair condition. Later we would find that the hide squared an easy nine feet and the skull measured 26 inches green, two points shy of making the Boone & Crockett record book.

We were curious as to the placement of the first two shots since both G.S. and Dennis had aimed for the head. After examining it closely we found that the stopping shot had smashed and severed the zygomatic arch, an outward arching, supporting bone structure starting at the base of the eye socket and curving down to the rear portion of the skull. The slug had struck an inch to the left of the bear's left eye socket. It wasn't a killing shot but apparently stunned or paralyzed the bear. The other slug had buried itself in the bear's right hindquarter.

Darkness accompanied the last hour of our hike back to the skiff and during the return trip with the 85-90 pound hide and skull, I was grateful for my familiarity with the inter-connecting deer trails. An hour and a half before midnight we reached the cabin.

Still hyped up by the charge, we had a bite to eat and over a cup of Scotch, tried to account for the bear's attack. An unprovoked brown bear charge is a rare occurrence.

The Kodiak National Wildlife Refuge has few recorded instances of bear attacks on man. In 1964 or 1965, Joe Want, now a guide, was coming home from a successful fox hunt in Olga Bay. He was walking on a willow and alder-lined bear trail when he came upon a sow with cubs feeding on fish. She attacked, and Joe fell into some grassy hummocks with his packboard sliding up to partially cover his head and neck. The sow bit into his packboard and arm once or twice and immediately departed with her offspring.

Another attack occurred in the fall of 1974. A boy about 15 years old and an older individual were deer hunting outside the refuge on the Shearwater Peninsula in Santa Flavia Bay. The boy was walking along a creek by himself and surprised a sow with three yearlings. She charged and he got off one shot before being hit. The sow departed without mauling him much. Alaska Department of Fish & Game officials looked over the site a day later and were unable to find any bear or blood sign.

Another attack occurred a few years ago when a man was mauled by a sow with cubs as he returned to pack out a deer that had been taken over by bears.

These incidents seem logical expressions of the bear's natural instincts, but our own and the next one were unusual.

In the fall of 1974, an amateur photographer was killed and eaten by a brown bear in the Izembek National Wildlife Refuge outside Cold Bay on the Alaska Peninsula. A search helicopter reportedly found the man's skull, a few bones, and some personal belongings. A brown bear was shot about 400 yards from the scene and the bear's stomach contained human remains. This bear was about five year old, healthy and a rabies test proved negative.

Most bear attacks seem to stem from an inadvertent mistake, like stumbling upon a bear kill, getting between or too close to a sow with cubs, or being attacked by a wounded bear. Even in the latter circumstance, the bear may be blindly trying to escape.

Perhaps the nine-foot bear that charged us had found a good feeding area and wanted to scare off the intruders, thought we were deer, or was curious at first and then so close he couldn't back down and still retain his dignity.

Another possibility is that he might have been a little cantankerous and we surprised him, thus providing sufficient grounds for attack. We'll never know for sure.

Admittedly not all brown bears are like this one and that's probably fortunate for hunters. But our experience and the other incidents demonstrate that the big bears are unpredictable and should never be taken for granted.

CHAPTER V

WORLD RECORD FOR A WEEK

Drawing a quick breath, I half whispered, "There he is."

Ron zeroed his binoculars on the big bull as he emerged wraith like from an alder patch.

Light rain drizzled from low gray clouds as we dug in on the grassy Alaska Range hillside and set up my spotting scope.

"Good points and long palms," I commented. "He's at least a 60 incher."

As Ron eased behind the scope and looked across the nearly alder encircled basin, I asked, "What do you think?"

The birch and willow leaves hadn't changed colors yet when Wisconsin bowhunter, Ron Kolpin, landed at our alder-lined, gravel bar strip along a tributary of the Yentna River, Alaska Range.

By late afternoon, Ron, vice-president of Kolpin Manufacturing Company (now president and producer of the Kolpin Modular Broadhead), had settled into our wall tent camp and taken some practice shots. Rain was pattering lightly on the tent canvas when the hissing Coleman lantern died for the night.

At a bleary eyed 4:50 a.m. breakfast, it was cloudy but not raining. After breakfast I saddled Poncho, Big Boy (a pack horse) and Ron's riding horse, a mare called April, among other things. Leaving camp we angled up-mountain behind camp and followed meandering moose trails through stands of spruce, birch trees and waist high, high bush cranberry bushes before encountering a wall of alders above timber line.

Tying the horses out, we fought alders for an hour before stumbling out and climbing a grassy ridge to glass for moose. A large black bear popped into sight briefly 200 yards away on a knob but we didn't have a chance to try for it.

We remained on the ridge all day, glassing grassy openings in the green-leafed alders for the tell-tale wink of flashing antlers. About 5 p.m. Ron spotted a cow and calf across the river near camp and just before we headed down I sighted a cow traveling through the timber but no bulls.

In the lantern-lit wall tent that night we sat around the wood stove and exchanged stories with my partner, Karl Braendel and his hunter, Clint List, a rifle hunter from New York. They had missed a black bear and spotted two bull moose, one in the 60 inch class but across a rugged, stream-gouged canyon that was uncrossable from their location.

The next morning, Karl's brother, Eric, went out to bring some horses in and spotted a nice bull nearby. He ran back to camp and a little later Clint collected a 56 6/8 inch bull.

After taking a look at Clint's bull, Ron and I headed upriver to hunt the swampy ridge between the impassable canyon and an alder-encircled basin where Karl and Clint had seen the estimated 60-inch bull the day before.

With Karl's words in mind, "When you spot a couple of cows you shouldn't have any trouble finding the bull as he's got a harem of four or five," I didn't think we'd have much trouble locating the bull.

We rode for two hours before staking the horses out along a

grassy meadow at the mountain base. Striking out on foot, we followed the right side of Bear Paw Creek, the creek that carved the uncrossable canyon. We followed moose trails part of the time and encountered one ravine with near vertical sides but managed to scramble up it, the thought of the big bull spurring us on.

An approaching wall of fog and rain from down-valley prodded us into quickening our pace. Two grassy and alder-patched rises later we reached the rim of the basin Karl had described and could see the ridge but not the swampy area on it.

Munching on a couple of candy bars, we mulled over our lack of choices for approaching the ridge crest. It would be useless and possibly costly climbing the ridge not knowing where the bull, if he was still there, was located.

Our only alternative was to fight through a densely covered alder slope on the basin's right side and gain enough height so we could glass the ridge top across the basin. Part way up the slope, light rain began falling and Ron slowed, traveling more carefully in order to protect his 62 pound Jennings Compound bow.

Over an hour had elapsed when I stopped a few yards ahead of Ron and spotted the big bull mentioned earlier.

After watching him a couple minutes, Ron took in the deteriorating weather situation and said, "Let's give him a try."

We side-hilled through dripping alders and circled toward the upper part of the ridge above the bull and his harem.

Pausing frequently to check on the bull, we noted that he was staying near a swampy pool below a large alder patch. It wasn't much to go on, for once we reached the ridge we'd be in chest-deep grass and alder thickets. One thing in our favor was that the bull was grunting occasionally, helping us to keep track of him.

An hour of working through alders brought us to a clearing on the upper ridge. A cow 300 yards away was looking in our direction so we halted briefly and rechecked the wind direction. The cow was angling slightly toward us, so when she lowered her head we hunched over and cut across the clearing.

Easing into some alders, we moved down and hit the swamp.

"There, there he is," I whispered to Ron, pointing to some exposed points in the alders 75 yards away.

Looking across the partially grass and swamp meadow, Ron's earlier words came strongly to mind, "In bowhunting the difference between 75 and 25 yards is not just 50 yards."

I sure wished he had a rifle at that moment.

Drifting down slightly until we were partially out of the bull's view, we lowered our packs and worked toward an alder patch closer to him. We stalked within 30 yards, the swamp squishing beneath our feet and the bull moved deeper into the brush. Ron stepped out into the clearing looking for a shot but the bull heard us and crashed through the alders.

Hardly pausing to be disappointed, we eased farther up and spotted the bull's antler tips again, jutting above the alder tops. Stalking him for the second time, we crossed another swampy section that threatened to suck our boots off.

Creeping ahead, we came to a narrow opening where I hoped we could sight the bull, but a cow was feeding there. Eyeball to eyeball with her, we froze and eased into a crouching position that we agonizingly maintained for several minutes, hoping the bull would appear. He did but crashed through too quickly for Ron to get a shot.

Rushing forward we went into the clearing and came out on the ridge overlooking the basin, just in time to see the bull heading toward the higher part of the basin where we had come from.

"We've got nothing to lose now, let's try and intercept him," I panted.

We ran back to the larger clearing and headed up the ridge. Hearts pounding, we pushed on and entered another small alley in the alders.

Stopping quickly, I motioned Ron to halt. "There he is," I whispered.

"Where?" Ron asked anxiously.

Slowly raising my hand I pointed at the antler tips exposed above the alders. Apparently the bull had circled back for his harem. We were 40 yards away but couldn't get a decent shot even though the bull could see us now.

He started walking and stopped in a moose-wide opening. Standing on his toes to clear some brush, Ron came to full draw and released his shot. To our chagrin the arrow swished under the broadside moose's head but he just watched it go by. Quickly nocking another arrow, Ron released again.

The yellow and white fletched arrow appeared to strike low in the moose's neck and we heard a thunk as it struck. Jumping, the bull crashed off toward the swamp. Running out of our alley we spotted him 100 yards off and Ron released another shot. I was amazed at how little a trajectory curve the arrow showed and at how close Ron came to the moving bull. His shot whisked by a couple feet in front of the moose's chest and the bull disappeared over a grassy rise.

Heading to the bull's last position we located a fair blood trail and began tracking. His trail passed near our packs and as I stooped over to pick them up I spotted the bull cutting back across the meadow 200 yards behind us. Whistling to draw Ron's attention, I motioned him to intercept the bull while I grabbed our packs. The bull crashed through a clump of alders like they didn't exist and headed down into the basin before Ron could get closer.

Continuing tracking, we found where the bull entered a good moose trail angling toward the base of the mountain. I figured he was feeling the effect of the arrow since he was heading downhill and following a good trail instead of trying to lose us.

Ron was leading in case we bumped into the bull, but still wasn't prepared when the bull crashed down the trail from an alder patch 20 yards ahead of us.

"Why don't we wait awhile and let him lie down?" he suggested.

His comment made good bowhunting sense, but I was

worried about losing the blood trail because we were finding coagulated blood. "I'm afraid if we don't push him farther we'll lose the trail and he'll disappear in the alders."

We decided to keep close until he reached timber-line. Continuing, we crossed a creek draining the brushy basin and spooked the bull again. He disappeared in some mixed birch and spruce tree stands. We listened intently and he stopped breaking brush fairly quick.

Sitting against a couple of birch trees, we ate a sandwich and forced ourselves to wait 20 minutes before following again.

Ron started out and I followed with my .338 Winchester magnum. A short distance down the bull's trail we found more blood sign where the bull had apparently stood for some time.

We cautiously moved on and Ron whispered, "What's that?"

A hoarse, rasping sound reached us and then we spotted the bull lying down 50 yards away. Using the cover of three spruce trees, Ron stalked within 25 yards and released an arrow.

To our amazement, the bull jumped up, ran about 50 yards before going down for good.

Upon examination, we discovered that Ron's first hit had been high on the fore-leg, not a good shot and we were fortunate to get him.

Darkness was nearly upon us and we were close to a quart low on blood from the biting flies and mosquitos by the time we opened the bull. Fortunately he had angled down-mountain within half a mile or so of the horses and we were able to reach camp shortly after dark.

In the morning we took two pack horses and retrieved the moose. It was a thoroughly miserable day and we were soaked when we reached camp.

The next day, Ron, an official Pope & Young scorer, and I rough scored his moose rack. We were astonished at the measurements; the spread was 62 1/4 inches, right palm width 14 3/8 inches, left 16 1/8 inches, right palm length 46 5/8 inches and the left went 45 inches. The total rough score minus differences was 224.

Ron had a card with P&Y minimum scores and records and according to it the world record Alaska-Yukon moose was held by William Wright with a bull taken in 1959 that scored 220 3/8.

We were stunned.

"A new world record," Ron mumbled. "And I almost passed him up because the hunt had barely started."

We celebrated that night to the accompaniment of Karl's brother, Gabe, and his guitar playing along with some medicinal spirits to combat the pouring rain pounding our wall tent.

A few days later we saddled up and with a packhorse rode upriver 20 miles to hunt caribou. As usual it was raining, pouring at times, and we made camp shortly before dark. After tying the horses out on a small hillside meadow, we crawled in for the night, wet enough to give the term, "wetback," a new meaning.

Rain continued through the night and we reluctantly crawled out in the morning to heed Mother Nature's call.

Shortly afterward the rain abated and we hiked up a nearby moose trail, slogging through dripping alders, and abruptly stopped when a 40 inch bull popped out of the alders with us. After seeing the moose we went farther and about 1 p.m. I spotted two caribou, and at first thought they were sheep because their manes were so white. They were quite away off and with the fog and rain we couldn't tell anything about their size.

About 4:30 we started back to camp and spotted 12 caribou close to where we'd spotted the others but lower. One was a nice white-maned bull with heavy, dark antlers.

"Let's go," Ron said without hesitation. "I'll take that one."

"I don't know if we have enough time before dark," I replied. "There's a heap of alder fighting before we can get there."

"They probably won't be there tomorrow though, will they?" Ron pressed.

"Okay," I said, knowing the futility but willing to give it a shot.

We turned back halfway there, lathered up like hard worked horses, and a bit worried about hypothermia since it had cleared off and we weren't sure about reaching camp before dark.

With a second effort spurred by hunger and thought of warm sleeping bags, we pushed hard for the tent. It was just shy of dark when we came down a ridge overlooking the meadow where the horses were.

I hollered to Big Boy, a tall white gelding, and asked him how he was doing. The words no sooner left my mouth when I noticed a bull moose, about a 40 incher, advancing on him and the other horses.

"Hey Ron, take a look at this," I said as he caught up with me.

"Get out of here," I yelled at the 300 yard distant bull as he moved closer to the horses.

The bull turned and ran toward the river but encountered a drop-off cliff, turned and charged back at the horses. I slammed a shell in my .338 and raised it as the bull closed within 35 yards of them. Still yelling, I started to squeeze off and the bull turned again, ran toward the drop-off and leaped off. He went completely out of sight in the river for a second before crossing it.

"Nothing to this caribou hunting?" I smiled at Ron later as we heated water for our freeze dried meals, our T-shirts steaming from the welcome heat. "It sure isn't the flatlands of the Peninsula (Alaska). "You'd think we were hunting Mountain caribou except that Alaska only has Barren Ground caribou."

Exhaustion zonked us out quickly and daylight had been around awhile before we stirred.

We scrapped a campfire together and did a bit of spotting as we dried our clothes, sighting a couple of black bear and a sow griz with two cubs on a nearby mountain.

Just before noon Ron spotted a band of caribou going over a mountain ridge but I only glimpsed the backend of one as they disappeared. They were quite away off but we headed after them anyway, the end of Ron's hunt was quickly approaching, only one more day of hunting remained.

Angling toward the caribou ridge we encountered a sheer-walled creek canyon and had to go up half a mile before crossing. A bit bushed already, we battled alders and willows for an hour before getting above the brush line and saw a nice bull moose in the 60 inch class briefly mount a cow in a clearing down mountain.

Halfway up the mountain, Ron was below me on a rocky bench as we looked for sign of the caribou but there wasn't anything recent, just old droppings and tracks. It was late so I whistled and motioned Ron to head back.

As I turned, something white in an alder patch two benches below Ron caught my eye, and I raised my binoculars.

"Caribou! A small one but maybe part of the herd," I thought.

I motioned Ron to halt and quickly skidded down to him. We eased over to the edge and spotted three more caribou, one a nice white maned bull.

"If we go after him we'll have to siwash tonight, there's no way we can make it back before dark," I said.

Ron took another look at the caribou, "Okay."

Checking the wind, we worked our way to the bench above them and Ron dislodged a large rock that bounced down a ravine right toward the caribou. Ron rolled his eyes in disgust and I shook my head, doubting the caribou would be there when we peeked over the edge.

The caribou had been lying down when we started after them but after the rock episode they got up and were feeding. Mentally wiping our brows in relief we got ready to resume the stalk in order to close the 250 yard distance so Ron could use his bow.

"Hold it Ron," I whispered and muttered. "Just our luck, a black bear is stalking them."

The caribou started getting jittery and more so when the bear disappeared in a nearby gully.

"If you want that bull you're going to have to use my .338," I advised.

Debating with himself a moment, Ron held out his hand and we stretched out prone.

"Hold midway on his shoulder," I said as Ron flicked the safety off.

At the first shot the bull anxiously looked down valley. Quickly chambering another round, Ron fired again and the bull crumpled, slid and rolled out of sight.

Slapping his back, I congratulated Ron on the shot, "Not bad for a rifle you've never fired."

It was 6 p.m. when we reached the bull and nearly dark by the time we caped and boned the meat. The black bear that had been stalking the caribou had not been affected by the shooting at all and was 300 yards away. Staggering down mountain a short distance to a rock ledge for a wind break, we hunted wood and managed to start a small, smoky alder fire.

Pouring rain wiped our fire out a bit later and we huddled beneath a space blanket the rest of the night. Whenever our chattering teeth prevented dozing I'd light a candle and we'd curl around it until our chattering ceased.

They say you learn more about a person on a short wilderness hunt than in a lifetime in a city, and that's true if you survive the night!

It cleared by morning and we stretched our frozen bones and started another small fire, glancing up at fresh snow 500 feet above us.

We were forced to climb back up with the caribou in order to get back, and by the time we flopped down at the tent I had to admit it was the toughest caribou hunt I'd been on.

A week after his moose and caribou hunt, at his Berlin,

Wisconsin home, Ron discovered his supposed world record moose had been surpassed by one taken by Dr. Michael Cusack of Anchorage, Alaska. Cusack's monster bull had 74 inch antlers that scored 248.

After drying and being officially measured, Ron's bull scored 219 and placed number five in the 1981 Pope & Young record book.

CHAPTER VI

ALASKA RANGE RAM

"I can't see him," Gloria anxiously whispered as she peered through her 4x Bushnell scope.

"Let's try another spot," I quickly suggested as she lowered her .270 Winchester. "We have to find a spot soon or it'll be too dark to shoot."

We elbowed along the rocky ridge, halted, and I raised my head an inch or two at a time until the gray shale slide below was visible.

"He's still there," I said as we paused to rest.

Gloria, my wife, needed a rest for the tough shot. Doubts flashed in her mind. "How can I shoot that far? Will the recoil knock me down the mountain?"

I was too busy trying to locate a shooting position in the disappearing light to ask what she was thinking then. My body was shivering with excitement and cold, and I doubted that 50 percent of the sheep hunters I've guided could have pulled this shot off. The full-curl-plus Dall ram was lying broadside on the shale slide 200 yards below us. The shot was nearly straight down. I didn't expect to find a shooting position, but sheep hunting is full of the unexpected.

We were hunting up a tributary creek valley of the south fork of the Kuskokwim River in the Alaska Range Mountains. The Alaska Range isn't as well known for producing large sheep as the Wrangells or the Chugach, but a few 40-inch rams seem to show up nearly every year.

Our trip had begun August 8 when Dave Gusse, our bush pilot, dropped us off in the Alaska Range on a narrow gravel strip. He would be back, weather permitting, 12 days later. We backpacked most of our second day to reach the creek valley where we set up a base camp. A freeze-dried meal recharged our bodies, and we climbed a ridge behind camp to do some glassing. Our efforts were rewarded with the sighting of three young rams across the creek.

With the season opening the next morning, we turned in at 9 p.m., thinking the sighting of three rams so close to camp was a good omen. Our spirits were dampened in the morning, though, because it was raining.

"Let's take enough food for a couple of days, our sleeping bags and space blankets, and look the area over." I suggested. "If the rams have moved, we'll move base camp."

We crossed the thigh-deep creek and ascended several spruce covered hills. Before leaving the tree line, we spotted a ewe and lamb along the creek and four young rams farther up the gorge. We angled up the mountain valley, battling through alder-choked ravines, and finally left the alders at 2,000 feet. At the same time, we angled into the main valley and lost sight of the Kuskokwim.

"Zeke! There's a sheep!" Gloria blurted out as we were crossing a steep, open slope. A lone sheep was feeding near an outcrop about 350 yards directly above us. I glanced up with my 7 x 35 Bushnells and saw horns.

"Down, get down," I said, motioning with my hand.

The slope was so steep we had to dig our toes in. I wiggled out of my pack and held it while Gloria pulled the spotting scope out.

"He's three-quarter curl on the side facing us," I whispered. We watched from our tenuous position for nearly ten minutes before the ram turned.

"Three-quarter curl," I said. "I was hoping he'd be seven-eighths and legal to shoot."

"I want a big one anyway," Gloria said with a smile. We waited until the ram fed out of sight, and then we sat up to hold a conference.

"There's a fair chance he might be near some others," I said. "It might be a good idea to backtrack, climb to the outcrop base, and work our way along it."

Two hours later, our legs were exhausted from zig-zagging up slides. Although I knew we could reach the outcrops, it would be impossible to circle the ram's position before dark.

"We'll have to look for a place to sleep," I said.

Gloria sat in a sheep bed while I climbed to investigate some possible sleeping areas, but none were level enough. Skidding my way back down, I sat beside her and said, "I guess we'll have to bivouac here."

"Won't we roll down the mountain?" Gloria asked as she stared at our hole in the ground.

"You can sleep on the inside," I joked. "Just don't thrash around or you'll be short a husband in the morning." She didn't smile.

Shortly after 5 a.m., we continued up the valley. An hour later, we had sighted nearly 40 sheep throughout the valley, although none were legal.

"Well honey," I said after a meager lunch, "it looks like we're going to have to head back because we're about out of food." We decided to climb higher on our way back and glass each time we rested.

"What are those two white spots?" Gloria asked, pointing

back up the valley.

"I saw two ewes and a lamb there earlier," I replied. But I pulled out the spotting scope anyway. I focused on the lower spot, and it was a white rock. The upper spot was at the base of a rugged cliff.

"The upper one is a ram," I said excitedly.

"How big?" asked Gloria.

"Can't really tell. He's looking right at us. But his horns are heavy," I said. "Jeez, he's a curl-and-a-quarter on one side."

"Let me see," Gloria pleaded. I reluctantly surrendered the spotting scope, and Gloria wistfully said, "Oh Zeke, I want him."

I didn't want to disappoint her, but the odds were against us. Our only chance was to cross a glacial canyon and climb the backside of several steep knobs to the left of the canyon. Then we could climb some rugged outcrops that would get us closer. But there would be open shale slides between us and the ram with no way to approach closer than 400 or 500 yards.

"Do you want to try it?" I asked. "It'll take about six hours to reach those rock outcrops." She looked at me, the ram, then nodded, even though she thought the ram would be gone before we got there.

We were in sight of the ram, so we continued up the mountain to set the ram's mind at ease, and then dropped into a tributary of the glacial canyon to head down and across. The narrow tributary soon became a series of dry waterfall drop-offs, and we were forced to climb out and snake our way through grassy hummocks to reach the main canyon.

We refilled our water bottle at the canyon creek and started climbing again, picking the best route to stay out of the ram's sight, which sent us up a near vertical wall. I was apprehensive about having Gloria climb it, but there didn't seem to be an alternative.

I made it, but had to drop to one knee a couple of times to

maintain my balance.

"Help, help me Zeke!" Gloria suddenly gasped. The rock studded slope slanted sharply into the boulder lined creek 30 feet below her. She was stuck, and the slope was slipping away beneath her feet.

I dumped my pack and eased down until she could reach my hand. Once safe, we rested until our hearts and her quivering legs calmed.

Then we started up the knobs. They seemed unending. We'd make 25 steps, rest while standing, and climb again. Finally, at 6 p.m., we were high enough to check for the ram.

"He's gone," I said, fatigue and disappointment etched on my face. "He must have fed around the mountain."

We continued climbing, glassing, and looking for a semi-level place to spend the night. At 8 p.m. we found a grassy spot and unrolled our sleeping bags.

"Do you want to crawl in now?" I asked, thinking if I was tired she must be exhausted. But I underestimated her desire to get the ram.

We left camp, climbed several more knobs, and glassed the slope on our left for the ram. On our right, the terrain dropped nearly straight off 700 feet to the glacial valley floor.

Stopping short of the last rock outcrop, we debated whether or not to continue since it was getting late and we'd have to climb around it on the dangerous side. It was jagged rock, but I could see some grass in a dip before the mountain became unclimbable.

We decided to take the gamble, and carefully crawled around the outcrop. A couple of steps ahead of Gloria, I spotted a patch of white 25 feet away. I nearly fell over backwards trying to stop. But it was only a weather-bleached caribou antler. We clambered down to the grassy dip, and I walked over to the shale slide side and looked down.

A ram — the ram — my binoculars confirmed was lying on the open slope 200 yards below us. But we couldn't find a spot to shoot from.

Finally improvising, we laid our coats over a rock and placed her rifle barrel on it. Then I stacked three large rocks under her left elbow. I sat partly in her lap, and she placed her right elbow on my shoulder.

"Okay, now aim about an inch up on him from the ground in line with his shoulder and neck," I advised. "That should compensate for the steep angle."

"I can see him in the scope now," she whispered.

"Now if you miss him and he runs right or left, don't forget to lead him a couple of feet," I added. "If he comes toward us, let him come as close as possible before shooting again."

I watched through my binoculars and she fired.

The ram's head slumped forward, he rolled over, kicked a couple of times, and slid 15 feet.

Stunned for a second, I jumped up and shouted, "You did it, and with one shot." I kissed her, and her face was one big smile.

We hurriedly zig-zagged our way down the slope, adrenaline still pumping. When we reached the ram, we admired him in silence a moment, and then I roughly measured the horns with my belt.

"He's around 37 to 38 inches with 12 to 13-inch bases," I happily said. I field-dressed the ram while Gloria steadied him, and we side-hilled it back to our camp in near darkness.

In the morning, we were surrounded by fog with visibility 200 feet or less. We waited a few hours, but at noon decided it wasn't going to clear. Loading our packs again, we started after the ram. An hour later we hadn't found him and weren't sure where we were.

"Maybe we dreamed that ram up," I said. Gloria gave me a look that said this was no time for joking.

A moment later a hole appeared in the clouds below us, and I saw three brown animals near some alders by the main creek.

I raised my binoculars and quietly said, "Grizzlies, a sow and two cubs."

"Oh no, I don't like this," Gloria moaned. "Are they going for my sheep?"

"Not very likely," I said. "At least not while the wind is blowing up the mountain."

We decided to climb to where she had shot and follow our tracks down. But we were farther off than we thought and couldn't find our trail. Angling farther up the valley, we bumped into our tracks and descended into the gray fog.

"There he is," Gloria breathed.

The fog was filled with mist, and our coats glistened with a watery sheen. The wind picked up, and Gloria held a space blanket for a wind break as I measured the ram's horns with a steel tape; they went 38 x 13 inches. I caped the ram, boned the front quarters, and left the hindquarters intact for packing.

It started raining before I finished, and we slipped our rain gear on. The long trip down the mountain with heavy packs wore out our legs, and it was almost dark when we reached the creek. Gloria was concerned about the grizzlies, and I have to admit I was wondering where they were, too.

We camped in some alders, and I set up a shelter while Gloria hunted for wood. It took me more than an hour to collect a large pile of shavings and get a smoky fire going. Later our jeans steamed as we huddled under the space blanket near the fire and roasted sheep tenderloin on a stick without benefit of salt and pepper.

Our down sleeping bags were wet in places but we crawled in to the accompaniment of the wind, rain, and a hissing, dying fire.

Rain was still drizzling and the clouds were halfway down the mountain when we rolled our sodden sleeping bags up and departed without breakfast at 8:30 a.m. Our food was gone, and we had been too tired to cook extra sheep meat the night before.

Our rest stops became longer and longer as we plodded along in hiking boots that squished with every step. Hours later we were on our way out of the valley.

About 7:30 p.m., after 11 hours of hard hiking, we spotted the blue dot that was camp. Our bodies were exhausted, but sighting camp gave us a boost. We stumbled into camp at 8:30, hung the meat, built a roaring fire, and ate until our bellies bulged.

The next day we dried our clothes and worked on the sheep cape. We headed out the following day. When we reached the small airstrip where we were to be picked up, I asked Gloria, "Do you really enjoy hunting?"

She looked down at the horns, broke into a smile, and then turned back to me. She didn't need to speak; the grin on her face answered my question. And it also reconfirmed the most important thing I'd learned on this trip: You don't have to fire a shot to bag a trophy. On this Dall sheep hunt, Gloria's smile was my trophy.

CHAPTER VII

THE GRANDDADDY OF ZACHAR BAY

Resting his battered gray spotting scope on a mossy hummock, Karl carefully focused. "I'll bet it's at least a ten-footer," he whispered.

Halfway up a nearby snow-capped mountain the biggest bear we had ever seen ambled uphill in a grassy clearing. Silver-gray hair on its back glistened in the early afternoon sun. Its enormous belly was unbelievable for a spring bear. And with the slow, deliberate motion peculiar to old trophy bears it ponderously moved into dense alders, pushing them aside as a battleship might cut through stormy seas.

We headed on an intercept course. Sweating so hard our eyeglasses nearly slid off, we half crawled and hauled ourselves through the thick alders. Rarely stopping, pausing only long enough to catch our breath, we pushed on.

Later that afternoon, with the sun making a hurried retreat behind the snowy white ridges, we dejectedly slogged back to camp. Our hunt was over. The Kodiak Airway's pilot was to pick us up in the morning.

"Sure wish we could have nailed that bear," murmured Karl. My thoughts exactly, but I mentioned that we had gotten one bear, and it had been a good hunt.

To most hunters the brown bear is a once-in-a-lifetime trophy, and we didn't look at it any differently. The only difference, perhaps, was that we wanted to hunt brown bear while we were young enough to make halfway good time in the mountains.

It was April 28, 1969, when we left the town of Kodiak in a chartered twin-engined Grumman Widgeon and headed for Zachar Bay, on the west side of the 103 by 57-mile island. A commercial fisherman and his wife accompanied us on the plane but got out at Larsen Bay, from which Zachar Bay was only a short hop. When told of our destination the man gave us some friendly advice: "Be careful, because that place really swarms with brown bears."

As the Widgeon lurched up on a gravel beach, we jumped out in hip boots and hurriedly unloaded our gear, then reconfirmed our pick-up date of May 8 with the pilot.

We were finally away from noisy cars, smog, and throngs of people in crowded cities. It was great to shoulder a pack again. For about the first mile, that is; then the 95-pound packs got heavy and we began looking for a base camp. Resting near a small, grass-bordered stream, we gulped down water so cold that our jaws ached.

Using a well-worn game trail, we climbed a brushy ridge and discovered a tiny clearing suitable for our camp. When the sun descended behind the mountains a chill crept into camp. Stoking our little camp stove, we devoured a four-man serving of chili from our dehydrated food supply.

Before turning in Karl spoke up, "You can take the first bear, since your hunting opportunities are almost zero in the Navy." Previously we had decided that if a brown bear was wounded and might escape into alders we'd both shoot.

Karl was using a Browning .338 magnum with 225 grain

bullets and I was using a Winchester Model 70 .338 with 300 grain handloads. Both guns were sighted in two inches high at a hundred yards. We also tried a few shots at 20 yards just to see how things would be if we ran into a bear at close range. For scopes, Karl was using a 4X Redfield, while I preferred a 4X Bushnell along with Pachmayr Lo Swing Mount, which in a tight situation would make my iron sights readily available. Karl and I believe that the .338 is the best all around gun for Alaska. A guide might prefer a little added insurance, but the average Alaskan hunter doesn't encounter many brown bears.

Sleep didn't come easily as we waited for morning, but we eventually drifted off.

We crawled out of warm sleeping bags early to be greeted by a blue sky stretching as far as we could see.

"Hmm, it got a bit cool last night," commented Karl, looking at the ice in our water pan.

Shouldering light packs, we set out for the beach. After an hour we encountered a rounded bump of land that protruded like a thumb a short distance into the bay. At high tide part of the arm was cut off and it was this part we walked up on. Sitting down to glass, we soon spotted a good-sized bear zigzagging its way up a mountain, plowing through the snow and alder patches. Its trail was easily discernable with binoculars and we watched until it crossed a high mountain pass. On the basis of seeing a bear from this rocky bump we named it "Bear Rock."

That day we did 13 hours of tough hiking in hip boots. Drenched in sweat we climbed halfway up a mountain to investigate some tracks we believed were fresh; well, they were fresh a couple of days earlier, anyway. (Now we consider tracks as fresh only if we see the bear making them.) Dragging into camp at nine o'clock we had some chow and passed out in our sleeping bags.

Exhausted, we didn't bother to get up until nine o'clock the next morning. Planning an easy day, we wandered up to Bear Rock. With old Sol beating down we continued glassing for bear. After awhile I tired of glassing, unlike Karl, whose binoculars seem to be an eye extension. It pays off though, especially in the number of bears he spots.

Rising, I half turned and a Sitka blacktail deer appeared like a magician's trick 100 feet away on the hillside behind us. Another deer appeared on the scene and the two approached within 25 feet. At the click of a camera shutter their ears snapped to attention while black nostrils quivered, but they didn't spook. Apparently without natural enemies except for the elements (brown bears would be hard put to catch one) they have done well since their introduction on Kodiak in 1924. Finally turning away, the two deer carefully stepped through the dead grass to the beach.

While watching the deer we glanced toward a partly open hillside 200 yards farther up the beach. My jaw dropped, "There's a bear!" We dropped cameras and hurriedly grabbed rifles. The bear was about 250 yards away and coming fast. Lying down we tensely waited. Karl whispered, "Looks fair-sized."

Suddenly plowing to a stop, it headed back up the hillside, apparently spooked from reflections off our rifles, or it was just being the usual unpredictable bear, as we were downwind. Stopping again, it reared up and began scratching its back on a scraggly spruce tree. With the crosshairs settled on its shoulder I started slowly squeezing the trigger. It dropped to the ground seconds before I could fire and loped off toward the alders. Holding just forward of the shoulder I touched off my .338, which halted the bear momentarily, just short of the alders. Then Karl fired seconds before it could disappear. Tumbling down the hillside it scrambled to its feet and headed back up.

Rapidly working my bolt, I cranked in another round and fired as it ran directly away from us. Then Karl's .338 fired and the bear fell again. Surprisingly it lurched to its feet and moved off slowly along small cliffs farther up the beach. Crashing through brush and threading its way among some trees, the wounded bear finally went down.

From our vantage point the animal remained partly visible as a shapeless clump of fur. After a short wait we moved in, knowing that we would soon lose sight of it.

Easing through dead grass and brush we moved up the hillside, passing the spruce where the bear had stood erect, like a man, to scratch its back. Just around another spruce tree we picked up the blood trail and slowly followed it through the brush, eyes and ears alert for any movement or sound.

"Stop, I see a brown patch!" whispered Karl. Motioning to his right he pointed into the crowded alders. I searched intently but didn't see anything.

Karl muttered, "I know I saw something but it's gone now."

The hair on the back of my neck wasn't standing up, but it didn't have far to go, because only 25 to 35 feet of partially clear area surrounded us. Pushing forward, every step we made sounded like a grouse bursting from cover.

Instant reflex action set in as my head cleared a small ridge and I saw the wounded brown bear. I slammed a shot into the bear's shoulder. Not over 25 feet separated us from the bear when it saw us.

Initially facing away the bear had swiveled its keg-sized head toward us and tried to struggle to its feet. It required four more slugs before it gave up.

"I've never seen an animal take that much lead and still live," Karl said in awe.

Skinning the bear we discovered a total of nine hits; five of which were more or less finishing shots. My first shot had hit in the fleshy part of the front shoulder and ranged forward into the neck. This shot probably accounted for the brown bear's lack of sound, for we never heard it growl. The bear had been hit twice in the hindquarters and one shot had hit low creasing its chest.

We were surprised that our boar was instead a large sow. Stretching the hide out we found it squared eight and a half feet.

This measurement was derived by measuring the open-skinned hide from nose to tail and then taking the width between the tips of the middle claws on opposite forelegs. Adding these two measurements and dividing by two gives the squared hide size.

We estimated a live weight of 700 pounds for the animal. It had a heavy, luxurious chocolate-colored fur.

For three days we regularly checked the bear carcass but no other bears appeared. During this time, bald eagles, ravens, and magpies reduced the carcass to a skeleton. One day we counted 20 bald eagles in the vicinity. Must have been a tough winter for them.

The last five days we put our binoculars on ten brown bears but they were generally inaccessible or disappeared before we could reach them.

It was our last day when we tried unsuccessfully for the Granddaddy of Zachar Bay. Later on Karl guided for Dennis Harms and took two hunters for brown bear in Zachar Bay, without seeing the old bear. He believes, though, that he saw the big fellow's tracks once.

Many years have drifted down the river now but the picture of the immense Kodiak bear is still sharp in my mind.

CHAPTER VIII

STRANGE YEAR OF ONE-ANTLERED MOOSE

Coming down a mountainous moose trail near Bearpaw Creek in the Alaska Range in 1974, Wisconsin hunter Ron Kolpin and I spotted a one-antlered moose in a clearing 100 yards away.

Two days later, Karl Braendel, and his New York hunter, Clint List, joined Ron and me upriver to search for caribou. Ron again spotted a small one-antlered bull in some alders. On their return trip, Karl and Clint spotted a third moose with a missing antler.

According to an Alaska Department of Fish & Game biologist, the sighting of three one-antlered bulls in one area is unusual, especially when the three different sightings were made along a 13-mile section of a river valley. In 30½ years of Alaska residency, I have only seen three one-antlered moose: these two in the Bearpaw Creek area, and one on the Alaska Peninsula in 1973.

All the one-antlered bulls we encountered had lost their

antlers right at the base. But when fighting, bull moose aren't always as fortunate. In 1968 Karl glimpsed a bull on the Alaska Peninsula with one antler intact and the other broken off about 12 inches from the base, with part of a jaggedly splintered palm still attached. It's hard to imagine the torque that must be exerted between two fighting, rut-incensed, 1,000-pound bulls before an antler splinters.

In late August the larger bull moose shed the velvet from their antlers and begin sparring with other bulls. Later they seek out single cows and breeding takes place from about September 15 to October 10, depending on the locality. These bulls usually drop their antlers during December and January; smaller bulls often retain theirs longer.

Bull moose, like deer, shed their antlers through a type of drying process. Hormonal stimulation, caused by a change in photoperiod (the interval in a 24-hour period during which a plant or animal is exposed to light), causes the cells to die. The shedding process is similar to that of leaves dying and falling off trees.

While checking my Alaska Range trapline in December 1974, I was able to partially date the antler shedding of one large bull. I discovered a half-buried antler just outside the protective limb canopy of a spruce tree on December 4. A snowfall of 2 inches had occurred during the evening of December 2 and a light layer had fallen the night of December 3. This skim of snow was the only coating on the exposed portion of the antler. This find was a fitting conclusion to a strange year of one-antlered moose.

CHAPTER IX

PONCHO-BUSH COUNTRY SURVIVOR

Few horses are kept in Alaska's Bush country due to difficulties and cost in caring for them. With the expenses involved, usually only horse-packing guides and outfitters can afford — often barely — to use horses.

My guiding area on the south side of the Alaska Range is marginal for horses because of the heavy snowfall accumulation. Horses can only forage in a limited way during the first couple of months of winter. With these conditions, horse feed must be flown in throughout the winter.

In November, 1977, my younger brother, Brian, nicknamed Farley, and I were trapping mink, marten, and wolverine along a tributary of the Yentna River and taking care of three horses used in my guiding operation. The horses, as well as the moose, were having a good year, with only a few inches of snow. We fed the horses before and after running our traplines, as it's important to maintain them in good shape before deeper snow and colder temperatures arrive.

The three horses, two mares and a gelding, named Mule, Punkin, and Poncho, respectively, foraged during the day and showed up fairly regularly for their twice-daily feeding of corn, oats, and barley mixed with complete horse feed in pellet form for roughage.

November 23 dawned clear and three degrees below zero when Mule and Punkin showed up at 7:30 for their morning grub. But no Poncho. When I climbed the steep bluff behind the cabin, I heard him whinny to the other horses and assumed he was all right. With good foraging conditions it wasn't unusual that the horses wouldn't show up occasionally, but in the evening Poncho still hadn't been seen.

"I'm a little worried about ol' Ponch," I said as Farley and I settled down to supper. "It's too late now but I reckon we better hunt for him tomorrow morning."

We skinned and stretched a couple of marten before bedtime and slept like hibernating bears.

In the morning no horses showed, and Farley said, "The horses have been traveling about half a mile downriver from the cabin, not far from my trapline. I'll take a look down there, but the area is really tracked up."

"I'll work my way down along the base of the bluff toward the area I heard Poncho yesterday," I replied. "If you find anything, yell and I'll do likewise."

Tightening the wool scarf around my neck in the nine-below weather, I headed out with Toklat, our summer bear dog. After half an hour of hiking I heard Farley's faint shout that he had found the two mares but no Poncho and that he would continue searching.

Nearly an hour had passed when Toklat angled out across a swamp-surrounded beaver pond. Suddenly I heard a whinny but couldn't pinpoint it.

"Ponch, where are you, boy?" I hollered.

I couldn't see anything even in that fairly open terrain.

Another whinny answered me, and I spotted a slight

movement on the far side of the beaver pond. I moved closer to investigate and gasped.

Poncho's head was sticking out of the beaver pond ice. With a lump in my throat I cautiously crossed the ice. Poncho turned his head toward me and whinnied again and again.

His back was partially out of the water and crusted with ice. He was shivering incessantly, and I grabbed some swamp grass which he chomped down quickly.

I yelled to Farley and waited while he headed over. The situation looked grim. We didn't have a come-along winch to pull Poncho out, and I wasn't sure he would have enough strength to help himself. Judging from the time he had whinnied the day before, he had been in there at least 24 hours.

We built two small fires to give him and ourselves an illusion of warmth. I stayed with Poncho while Farley ran back to the cabin for some burlap bags, rope, and two axes.

Poncho was only a few feet from the edge of the beaver dam, but it dropped sharply there. We decided to chop an opening to the dam and try to lead him out.

Alternating turns chopping, we spent an hour cutting a channel before it was wide enough to try. I tied a bowline around Poncho's neck and we tugged on the rope.

"Come on. Ponch, come on, boy, you can do it," we coaxed.

He struggled unsuccessfully as we increased our pulling efforts.

Suddenly Poncho staggered out, stumbling on his knees, as we continued pulling. He nearly went down, but kept his balance and came to a spraddle-legged stop.

We rubbed him with our bare hands to get as much excess water off as possible, and then used the burlap bags. He wouldn't roll in the snow, so we led him to the cabin, occasionally trotting him to improve his circulation.

At the cabin we used a roll of paper towels to dry him better, and he rolled once while we rested. When he got up we put two saddle blankets and a saddle on him. We considered bringing him into the cabin, but he stopped shivering and seemed anxious to join the other horses, so we let him.

We worried for a couple of days that he might get pneumonia, but he pulled through in fine shape. It was the happy ending of what could have been a tragedy for our favorite horse.

CHAPTER X

TEN FEET TO OBLIVION

"That lower one is big," I said as we eyeballed two Mountain goats through the spotting scope. "Looks like a nanny but the horns are well over nine inches, maybe even ten."

"The horns are definitely longer than her face," I added.

From our angle the goats were on an inaccessible, grass-edged cliff with the larger one lying down and idly swinging a front leg over a 500 foot drop. We slipped back behind our vantage point, a steep, glacial moraine pile, and held a consultation.

My hunter, John Babler, a stocky built fellow from White Bear, Minnesota, was in Alaska to hunt Dall sheep. If successful, he would be halfway to a grand slam, having previously taken a Stone sheep in British Columbia. While there he had run out of time for taking a Mountain goat and hoped to get one this trip.

It was September 1972 and the last hunt of the season in this area, since winter storms hit early along Alaska's Chitina Glacier, deep in the Wrangell Mountains. This area contains some of the roughest hunting terrain in Alaska.

"I'd sure like to get a shot at that big goat," John said as we talked over the possibilities.

"Let's hike farther up-valley, maybe we can find a better route up the mountain," I said hopefully.

We slipped our packs on and weaved between the moraine piles of the near vertical walled tributary valley to the crevassed Chitina Glacier.

The goats spotted us but didn't seemed concerned.

Two days earlier, John and I had reached our spike camp with another assistant guide, Doug McRae and John's partner, Dan Gillner, an airline pilot. We stayed the night there and separated in the morning. John and I headed up the narrow glacier valley while Doug and Dan headed up the main glacier.

During the next 13 hours, John and I spotted two bands of rams with four sheep each. Spooky from nearly a month of hunting pressure, they quickly disappeared in side canyons after sighting us. One had been a nice ram with 37 to 38 inch horns and heavy bases.

Resting on a rock pile on our way back to spike camp, John suddenly said, "I see a wolverine."

I turned and spotted the animal angling across the base of an alluvial slide.

"That's the biggest wolverine I've ever seen," I smiled as I studied it through my binoculars.

It was an estimated eight foot grizzly, chestnut brown with blond tipped guard hairs. Through my spotting scope the bear's ivory claws appeared as long as dinner knives, by far the largest I've ever witnessed on a bear. We watched the grizzly cross some deep cut ravines and disappear in a rocky area halfway up a rugged mountain.

"Maybe that's what spooked the four sheep on this side of the valley," John commented.

At spike camp that night we decided to take our sleeping bags with us the next morning and save some hunting time.

Zeke, on left and Karl Braendel, approach Zeke's Kodiak brown bear. It's wise to come in above a wounded bear whenever possible as you never know when you might need that extra edge.

Zeke, on left, and Karl Braendel with the tough bear's hide. The punishment these big bears can aborb is amazing and must be taken into consideration when choosing an approprate rifle for hunting them. This 8½ foot sow was taken along Zachar Bay in 1969 on a spring hunt.

Allan Leary of Dawson, Yukon Territory, looks over the aftermath of a Kodiak brown bear fight near Uganik Bay, Kodiak Island. The loser, an estimated nine foot bear that was later aged at 11 years old, lies in the foreground. The bear had been partially buried and the broken alders and flattened ground testify to the intensity of the fight that occurred in early May 1984.

Slightly sun melted tracks of a ten foot Kodiak bear resemble dinosaur tracks in the snow. Canadian hunter, Allan Leary checks tracks out, hoping to find a bear with tracks like it.

An estimated 7½ foot sow Kodiak brown bear near Uganik Lake, Kodiak Island. When these bears come out from hibernation they search for roots and new grass, being omnivorous rather than true predators like the African lion.

Bill Sanders of Washington, Pennsylvania, with a nice brown/grizzly bear taken with one shot from .60 side by side double rifle (muzzleloader) built by John Cunningham of Uniontown, Pennsylvania. In 1981 this bear was the world record in the primitive arms division of the Burkett Trophy Measuring System.

An idyllic base camp in the rugged sheep country of the Wrangell Mountains near Chitina Glacier. Photo taken in September 1973.

A nice Sitka blacktail buck taken near Uganik Bay by Tony LaRoma of Richland, Michigan with a .340 Weatherby at 100 yards. Sitka blacktails were introduced in the mid 1920's and early 30's and are doing well on Kodiak with a generous bag limit of five in most places.

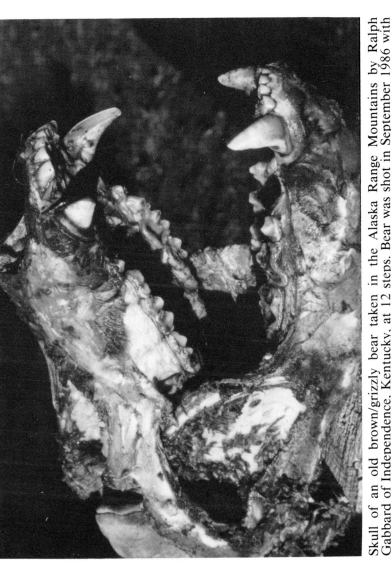

Skull of an old brown/grizzly bear taken in the Alaska Range Mountains by Ralph Gabbard of Independence, Kentucky, at 12 steps. Bear was shot in September 1986 with "Afrique," Zeke's .338 Sako that accompanied him to Africa. Ralph didn't have time to use his own rifle as the bear was coming toward us, down a hill, not charging but walking. Bear was a sow that squared 7 feet. Note the broken fang and decaying molars.

Packer, Allen Huling of Kodiak, and Zeke take a breather on a backpack hunt for Kodiak brown bear on the west side of Kodiak Island. Note the well worn bear trail they're following. Photo by Dr. Tim Norris.

Packer, Allen Huling of Kodiak, Island, on left and Zeke with 9'8" Kodiak brown bear taken by Dr. Tim Norris, an Army major stationed in Honolulu, Hawaii.

Dr. Tim Norris of Honolulu, Hawaii, on left, waits patiently as Zeke works on late breakfast after getting bear the day before on the west side of Kodiak Island in May 1987. Photo by Allen Huling.

Dr. Tim Norris, an Army major stationed in Honolulu, Hawaii, with his 9'8" Kodiak brown bear taken from Rohrer's Bear Camp on a backpack hunt on the west side of Kodiak Island. Bear was taken the first part of May 1987 with one shot from a Ruger .338 (two insurance shots were fired but not necessary).

An unusually colored, very light, sow Kodiak brown bear taken by Allan Coranet of Cincinnati, Ohio. This eight foot bear took three solid shots from a .375 and two .338 rounds before expiring.

Bob McCutheon of York, South Carolina, on left and Master guide, Zeke, with Bob's ten foot brown bear taken from Rohrer's Bear Camp on the west side of Kodiak Island. Bear scored 27 11/16 and was taken the spring of 1987.

Zeke with a fair caribou that he took on a short hunt near Ugashik River, Alaska Peninsula, in the fall of 1972. Photo by Ben Guild.

Montana hunter, Jack Geiger, watches Zeke cape his high country Sitka blacktail buck taken near Uganik Bay, Kodiak Island in the fall of 1985. Photo by Dave Hall.

A well haired fall Kodiak brown bear taken by Tony LaRoma of Richland, Michigan. It's unusual to take a bear this high up in the fall and it took us nearly an hour to stalk from 400 to 200 yards in the open country before the bear started to spook. Bear took several shots before succumbing and squared 8½ feet. A long climb from tidewater along Uganik Bay was necessary to reach the bear.

Typical alder brush terrain surrounds an estimated 7½ foot Kodiak bear near Uganik Lake, Kodiak Island. Working a good shot through brush like this can be difficult and the first shot is most important.

Zeke goes in after a wounded grizzly in the Alaska Range Mountains. Tracking a wounded bear in this type of terrain can be hazardous and possibly fatal, emphasizing the need for proper first shot placement. With brush like this it's impossible to parallel the trail looking for an ambush, you have to stay on the trail. Photo by Dale Langkilde.

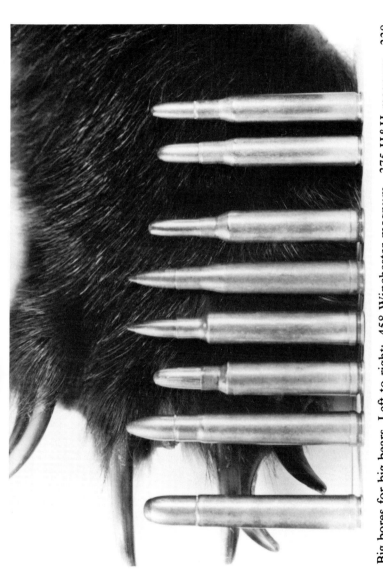

Big bores for big bears. Left to right: .458 Winchester magnum, .375 H&H magnum, .338 Winchester magnum, .300 Weatherby magnum, .300 H&H magnum, 7MM magnum, 30-06, .270.

Zeke with hide of six foot black bear taken at 18 steps with a Ruger .41 magnum pistol. Bear had destroyed some insulation, tar paper, a window and eaten half a bag of dog food. This bear returned when author was burning some of the garbage. Bear was shot in June along Skeeter Lake in the Alaska Range Mountains.

When first light crept in I poked my head out the three man tent door and discovered that a dense layer of clouds and fog reached halfway down the mountains. Next to rain and snow this is one of the worst developments for sheep and goat hunters, as it's tough to hunt when you can't see.

After breakfast, John and I reached the valley mouth in an hour, the hike warming our chilled bodies. As we continued up-valley the cloud cover began breaking up.

It was early afternoon when we sighted the two mountain goats mentioned earlier. The smaller one appeared to be a seven inch billy.

Shortly afterward we located a possible route to the goats that would keep us out of sight as we stalked them. But getting off the glacier proved to be a challenge until we discovered a low ice ridge, slid down it, crossed an ice-bottomed creek, and climbed a 20-foot, rock speckled ice ridge to the mountain base. We gradually angled up, climbing some cement like mud slides.

After an hours' climb we reached a series of grassy sections that zig-zagged toward the goats. It was steep but relatively easy going and we pushed ourselves until dry-mouthed.

"I sure hope they're still there," John panted.

After another hours' climb we quietly chambered a round and cautiously crawled to a cliff edge that I figured should put us in shooting range.

"There's one," John breathed as he shouldered and pointed his .300 Weatherby down at a 75 yard distant goat.

I subconsciously checked to see whether or not we could retrieve the goat after shooting and checked it through my binoculars.

"Hold it, hold it John, that's not the big one," I snapped.

This goat was part-way out from the cliff face and the other one wasn't visible.

I snaked forward to the right and spotted the larger goat feeding on a grassy ledge below a series of rounded rock cliffs.

John joined me after I signaled him and we waited a few minutes until the goat moved out from the cliff face. It was looking down-valley and standing on a relatively level but small, grass ledge.

"Shoot it through the front shoulder," I advised as John prepared to fire. "Hopefully that will anchor it."

As John's shot echoed through the canyons, the mountain goat dropped but still had it's head up. Through my 7X35 binoculars, blood was visible on the front shoulder.

"Shoot again," I said, shaking my head in wonderment at the goat's toughness.

With this shot the goat lurched forward, reflexively kicking and flopped off the ledge. Our hearts popped into our mouths as we watched the goat roll an agonizing six feet before stopping four feet from the cliff edge and oblivion.

The sheer fall to the glacier likely would have destroyed the horns since they are notoriously more fragile than sheep horns.

After wiping the sweat from my brow, I laid my .338 down and edged down the cliff at the best place I could find. The first third of the decent wasn't bad, but as I continued it became increasingly difficult, making me shift back and forth laterally to find finger and foot holds.

I was easing along a small ledge when the shadow of a goat's head appeared on the smooth cliff face 75 feet from me and on the same level. My heart ceased functioning momentarily and I began slowly backtracking, not wishing to meet a goat at arm's length or feel the stilleto sharp horns.

Mountain goats aren't considered dangerous but they can kill other goats. And Andy Russell, in his fine book, "Grizzly Country," described an incident in which a goat met a grizzly on a narrow ledge and buried it's horns in the bear's chest. The grizzly killed the goat but subsequently died, as one of the goat's horns had reached it's heart.

"Don't think I can get down that way John," I said breathlessly as I climbed back. "Besides, that other goat is down there."

We traveled along the cliff-edge searching for a better route down. Finally I pulled my 3/8 inch nylon line out of my pack and John anchored it around a rock and let me down a near vertical 15 foot section to a grassy ledge. Untying the rope I crossed a dangerous rock area, shaped like the top of a baseball and only offering a few narrow cracks for holds.

A few harrowing minutes later I reached the goat and measured the long, narrow horns.

"It's a nanny and the horns go 9 3/4 inches," I hollered to John.

I partially caped the goat and loaded my pack with it and the boned meat. Then I carefully crossed the rock dome, tied my pack to the rope and John pulled it up. He lowered the rope again and drug me a short distance until I could gain some purchase with my hands and feet.

"Jeez, I hope you don't have to do this for every goat you take," John commented.

"This wasn't my worst one but it ranks right up there," I smiled as we headed down.

Halfway down a grassy slope we suddenly sighted two sheep, only partially visible and 200 yards below us. Flattening against the slope, I quickly scanned them with my binoculars. Both were young rams just under the legal minimum of 3/4 curl (now 7/8 curl requirement).

Darkness was approaching when we reached the glacier and we tried unsuccessfully to beat it. On a semi-level, rock infested moraine we stretched out a space blanket, unrolled our sleeping bags and spread a condensation gathering nylon tarp over our bags in case it rained. At the first suggestion of dawn we were awake and gladly departed our make-shift camp.

Back at spike camp we hung the meat and devoured a pancake breakfast. I finished the goat cape just before Doug and Dan came in with a beautiful 41 inch ram they had taken with little climbing.

We exchanged hunting tales and they told us about a dark

horned ram that would go an estimated 38 inches.

"He's about halfway up a mountain on the left side of a long narrow gorge," Doug said. "All you have to do is find the camp and look up by a large white rock. The ram doesn't seem to move more than 50 yards from it. Then zig-zag up some greens, go up a chute and you've got him; nothing to it," he laughed.

John and I would remember those words of understatement.

We left the spike camp at 3 p.m. and barely found the spruce tree and brush surrounded campsite by nightfall.

Early the next morning we cautiously crawled out into a small clearing and searched for the ram. Sure enough, he was feeding near a white rock but above him in some unclimbable cliffs were two estimated 40 inchers and a 3/4 curl ram.

"Sure like to get one of those big boys but I'm not sure we can even get to the lower one," I said.

Soon after we started I broke out my 50 feet of climbing rope for safety. We attached it with bowlines around our waists and John gave me slack as I climbed. Since he was 30 pounds heavier than me, I figured he'd make a good anchor if I slipped. Near the rope's end I'd find a place to anchor myself and take up the slack as John climbed.

After a rocky stretch we'd occasionally come out on a grassy area and rest.

As the morning progressed the air currents began warming and rising, carrying our scent straight up the mountain toward the sheep. We had planned on following the grassy areas as much as possible but this event forced us to alter plans and travel closer to the gorge.

We slowed down as the climbing became tougher and I had to backtrack several times.

"Make sure you anchor yourself good," John commented as he prepared to climb a loose rock area. "Hate to see us go back down the mountain like a bola."

He reached me and I smiled and said, "I'm not worried about that, you thought I tied a bowline around my waist, actually

I've got a quick release slip knot. That way if you fall I can release you, no use in both of us going."

He laughed, but took a sideways glance at my knot as we rested on a dirt covered ledge.

A total of four hours had elapsed when we reached a cliff that I figured was a little over three-quarters of the distance to the ram. Thirty feet high, it offered three chutes as choices to climb, otherwise we'd have to cross a grassy stretch and risk exposing ourselves to the sheep or being scented.

I tried two chutes and climbed within a few feet of the crest before failing, and had an exciting time returning.

"Might as well give it up and head back down," a worried John said. "It's getting pretty dangerous."

"We've made it this far, might as well try the last one John," I said, taking a deep breath.

I used every available niche and projecting rock and managed to work myself within five feet of the top. Testing an essential rock, I felt it come loose slightly in my hand. It was tough avoiding it and with a mouth as dry as desert sand I warned John to watch for it on his way up. Finally, with a last scramble I pulled myself over the edge.

I rested in the bunch grass a couple of minutes, braced my feet and told John, "It's not bad, you'll make it all right."

After we scaled that cliff and rested, the climbing became easier.

Our fifth hour on the mountain had passed when I figured we were close to the ram.

"Untie your rope and go ahead," I whispered. "He might be just over that rise in front of us."

Slipping a round into the chamber, John crawled forward to peer over the rock-strewn, grassy slope above us.

His head barely cleared it and he instantly dropped back.

"He's looking right at me," he gasped.

I quickly shuffled forward and John flopped into shooting

position and fired at the 80 yard distant ram. The ram's hindquarters sagged and it's head wobbled. John shot again and blew up a rock 20 feet in front of us that hadn't been visible in the scope.

A red blotch appeared just in front of the ram's hindquarters and he keeled over, started sliding and rolling.

I sprinted toward the animal with rope in hand and John cut across to the left on an intercept course. The ram tumbled onto a rockslide and I winced inwardly as it picked up speed and passed me.

Fifty feet below me the ram caught momentarily on a large rock and started kicking with one foot.

Leaping down the slope I reached it and threw two quick wraps around a front leg that would have done justice to a rodeo calf roper using a pigging string. Like the Mountain goat, another 10 feet and the ram could have rolled into oblivion.

Out of breath, I braced myself against the slope and waited until John joined me before dragging the ram to a better place to work on it.

The heavily broomed veteran was over ten years old and only had five teeth remaining. His left horn measured 33 1/2 inches, the right 34 1/2 and the bases were 13 1/2 inches. The dark horns had been deceptive in length, but the ram was a fair chase trophy in the truest sense. And it's doubtful that he would have survived another winter.

Our return trip was easier but we still had to use the rope two times and stumbled into camp by feel.

Rain woke us the next morning and I felt thankful that we hadn't been stuck on the cliffs overnight and forced to descend the rain slickened mountain that day.

Eight hours of monotonous, gruelling glacier travel later we reached base camp.

The next day Doug and I returned to the spike camp and backpacked the remaining gear and John's goat to base camp.

We were flown out September 9 and when we shook hands

John said, "I'll never forget the memories of our hunt."

I felt the same way; it's not always the biggest trophy that instills the best memories, but the adventures and companionship along the trail.

CHAPTER XI

BLACK BEARS OF PRINCE WILLIAM SOUND

Feeling a nudge, I opened my eyes to see the tent wall wavering. Bruce reached over me and grasped Karl's .44 magnum. He held one finger to his lips.

"That bear batted the packboard I was sleeping against," Bruce tensely whispered. Pistol in hand, he carefully unzipped the tent door and froze — nose to nose with a big, dripping-wet black bear.

With one thunderous blast from the .44 magnum, Bruce dropped it at six feet.

I don't think Bruce had reckoned on this much excitement when he decided to take leave from the Navy in May of 1969 for a black bear hunt in Alaska with me. My Alaskan hunting stories had helped us pass monotonous hours of radar watch while cruising toward Southeast Asian waters. Enthralled by my numerous bear tales, Bruce wanted an animal badly, so I rashly guaranteed him a black bear in a part of Alaska largely untouched by hunters.

Twenty-one years old at the time, Bruce Jay Thomas, or B.J., was from Fulton, New York, where he regularly hunted deer before joining the Navy in January, 1967. An avid sportsman, he often reminisced about the bird and deer hunting he had enjoyed in New York.

Karl Braendel, then 21, the third member of our hunting party, lived at Eagle River, his birthplace, a small community 15 miles from Anchorage. While B.J. and I pulled leave from the Navy, Karl managed a leave of absence from his job with a printing company in Anchorage. An enthusiastic hunter, Karl had collected specimens of many of Alaska's big game species, including a Rocky Mountain goat and caribou that narrowly missed the Boone & Crockett minimum scores.

At the time of the hunt I was 20, and living a few miles from Eagle River, in Chugiak, another small community. With only nine days of leave left, I was off bear hunting again, much to my mother's consternation. Just a few days earlier, Karl and I had completed an 11-day brown bear hunt on Kodiak Island, where I succeeded in bagging a bear that squared eight and a half feet.

When B.J. arrived at the Anchorage International Airport on May 14, Karl and I were there to meet him, and early the next morning, Karl, B.J. and I arrived at Jim's Flying Service, which operated out of Lake Hood on the outskirts of Anchorage. Our prearranged destination was Siwash Bay in Prince William Sound. Our pilot, Ketch Ketchum, was to take us there in a Cessna 185.

Flying east from Anchorage above muddy Cook Inlet, we headed for Portage Glacier Pass. Suddenly in thick cloud cover, we were forced to fly short spirals in order to avoid a mountain. Noticing a break in the clouds, Ketch flew an alternate route over the snowy Chugach Mountain Range.

Nearing the end of Esther Passage in overcast Prince William Sound, we spotted a strolling black bear on a snow-free beach. Karl and I were apprehensive about the still-deep snow in most areas. In early spring bears usually forage along beaches in search of easily accessible food.

We circled over Siwash and adjacent Eaglek Bay, then changed our minds and decided on Eaglek for the better hunting area it offered. As we taxied to the beach, I stepped out on the plane's right pontoon and saw a sudden movement. Backgrounded by dense spruce forest, a black mink loped toward us; suddenly pausing, it checked out the noisy intruder before disappearing into the brush. We unloaded our gear, and Ketch left for Anchorage.

Finding a camping place was a problem, for dense forest fenced off the beach except for a small strip above high-tide mark. Using what was available, we erected our three-man tent on an inclined grassy spot below a small, snow-covered ridge.

In the misty morning of the next day, we hunted the beach in our immediate area. B.J. carried a scope-sighted 7 mm Remington magnum that he had purchased in Hong Kong. Factory 175-grain bullets constituted his bear loads. Karl and I toted our scope-sighted .338's; mine, a Winchester Model 70 with 4x Bushnell and his, a Browning with 4X Redfield. We both handload. I favor 250-grain Hornaday bullets backed by 72 grains of 4831, while Karl has had more success with 225-grain bullets and 72 grains of 4350.

In two days of hiking and concentrated glassing, we saw but one fair-sized blackie. To fire a shot at that bear, we would have had to make a two-day hike along the bay. We were forced to confine our hunting to the beach at low tide because of the deep snow.

Third day out, we hunted in bright sunshine. Moseying down the beach, we finally hiked up a shallow, gravel-bottomed stream entering the bay. The streambanks were blanketed with three feet of semi-packed snow, but the stream allowed us access into the valley. A short distance upstream, we discovered bear tracks.

"Looks like they were made last night," commented Karl.

The frozen tracks paralleled the stream for 30 yards. While checking them for freshness, we located a pile of frozen bear dung, which further convinced us not to try and track the black bear down.

Rounding a stream bend farther upstream, we were greeted by a small, rugged glacier situated at the valley's head.

"There's a bear," grunted Karl suddenly.

Thrusting our light packs in the snow, we watched the animal through binoculars as it wandered aimlessly in search of newly sprouted plants.

"We might as well head straight up the stream valley," suggested Karl. "Then we'll have the wind in our faces. We can walk on the snowslides, and the stream will help mask our approach."

"Sounds good," added B.J.

Staying as low as possible, we headed for the base of a snowy ridge that would place us about 100 yards from the unsuspecting blackie. We arrived undetected and crept to the crest.

"There it is!" whispered B.J.

Stretching prone, B.J. settled the crosshairs of his 4x Weaver scope on the black bear's shoulder and waited for it to clear a sparse clump of alders. Luckily, the bear had moved only a short distance from where we had originally sighted it.

Lurching from the impact, the bear headed uphill. B.J. hastily chambered another round and fired again. We heard the bullet strike home, but the black bear continued up. Firing again, B.J. missed. With his next shot the bear collapsed.

Congratulating B.J., we snapped some pictures and skinned the bear, a nice sow that squared five feet.

Karl and I consider black bear meat pretty decent fare, so we hauled along one hindquarter, the backstraps and tenderloin. Alaskan law doesn't require salvaging bear meat as long as the hunter recovers the hide.

Next day, May 18, B.J. and I hunted the valley again, while

Karl hunted the beach. Hiking out of the valley at seven o'clock in the evening, we happened to glance back and spot a bear. Darkness doesn't set in this time of year until about 10 p.m., so we had nearly three hours of daylight remaining. I figured it would take us an hour to reach the bear.

"Do you want to go after it?" I asked.

"Yeah," replied B.J. with eyes riveted to binoculars.

While observing the black bear I said slowly, "If we do, there's a good chance we'll be siwashing tonight."

"That'll be all right," commented B.J.

"Well, we better get in gear then," I ventured.

Scrambling up the snowslide where we had last seen the black bear, we looked for tracks. Finally I found them in soft thigh-deep snow at the slide's edge.

"Hmm, they're pretty small," I grunted.

But we pushed on, hoping to get a glimpse of the bear. Suddenly spotting it, I rapidly shouldered my rifle, locking the intersecting post and crosshairs of my scope on the bear's shoulder. But shooting offhand at about 300 yards while standing in deep snow, seemed to push my rifleman abilities too far. Reluctantly lowering my .338, I watched the bear slowly amble over a distant ridge.

Wearily we headed into a ravine which lead to the valley floor. A third of the way down, we glanced back up the mountain. In the rapidly fading light we spotted our bear with two other furry bundles at the base of a steep cliff. The two cubs held an impromptu boxing match, then proceeded to pester their mother until she pinned one and knocked the other rolling.

A queasy feeling came over me as I realized that I unknowingly almost sentenced the two cubs to perish of possible starvation.

After slogging down to the stream mouth, we discovered the tide had rolled in during our absence. We pushed on in the darkness along 30-foot cliffs bordering the bay. Much swearing accompanied our sliding, falling progress toward camp.

Jokingly, I asked B.J. what he thought of Alaskan hunting now but only received some muttered under-breaths.

In camp we were greeted by a yawn from Karl and a, "Soup's on." With food our fatigue seemed to disappear. Nestled snugly in my sleeping bag, I thought of our hunting area.

Prince William Sound is one of the unsung black bear hunting areas in Alaska. Alaskans in general consider this bear more of a varmint than big game. No closed season on blacks exists in 18 of Alaska's 26 hunting units. Of the black bears taken, many are bagged incidentally by hunters tracking other big game species.

In most of Alaska the bag limit is three bears, excluding sows with cubs. The present limit in Prince William Sound is one bear although it was two at the time of our hunt. The limit in Southeast Alaska is two.

With continued hunting pressure from the southern 48 states, it seems likely that black bear hunting will someday overshadow that for the less numerous brown and Grizzly bears which are getting increasing protection.

The next morning we were shocked to discover that the black bears of this part of Alaska can be quite bold, indeed.

"Damn! Another bear snuck off with our meat!" yelled Karl, "and judging by his tracks, a big one."

Karl had placed the hindquarter from B.J.'s bear in a snowbank near camp. Sometime during early morning we heard a slight rustling sound but didn't bother to investigate.

As we studied the thief's tracks, it started raining. It rained continually until our departure some 62 hours later.

The next morning we were awakened again by a scraping against the plastic tarp stretched from our tent to the hillside. Slipping Karl's easily accessible Ruger .44 magnum from its holster, I held it tightly in one hand and slowly opened the tent door. I didn't see anything as I peered through the opening.

"Must have been that same bear," murmured Karl sleepily.

With the rain's accompanying patter, we lit our little single-burner Coleman and cooked bacon and pancakes. Being tentbound by the unexpected rain, we needed some amusement to help pass the time. Tearing up some notebook paper we put together a deck of cards and played casino most of the day.

Blackie must have thought it was an all-nighter, for he dropped in early that morning to join the game, but was destined to end up on B.J.'s floor as a trophy rug.

"Wonder if that nosey bear will come back?" B.J. pondered.

Seven o'clock the morning of the 23rd he got his answer.

With the tent door partially unzipped and nose-to-nose with our bold black bear, B.J. fired. At that moment, with the confined blast of the .44 ringing in my ears, I was hoping the bear would drop in its tracks and wouldn't try to demolish the tent and its inhabitants. Blackie obliged. He never moved again because B.J. had slammed a 240-grain slug just over his eye.

Skinning out the bear in drizzling rain was unpleasant, but it would have taken a tidal wave to dampen B.J.'s spirits.

"Back in New York the folks will never believe this!" he happily exclaimed while looking down at his second bear, a boar which squared out just short of six feet.

"That's for sure! When bears start coming into camp, you've found a pretty good hunting area," I said.

Prince William Sound is prime black bear territory, with one notable exception, Passage Canal, just out of Whittier, a small port town, where the bears have been heavily hunted. Some good nearby areas to consider are Esther Passage, Eaglek Bay and Culross Passage.

To reach Prince William Sound hunters from the lower 48 could drive to Anchorage via the Alaska Highway and charter a small plane from one of the numerous flying services at Anchorage, as we did.

Another possible route is by Alaska's Marine Highway System. A sportsman can board a ferry at Seattle or Prince Rupert, British Columbia, and get off at Haines, Alaska, and complete the drive to Anchorage. This eliminates some rough, gravel-road driving and enables hunters to see Alaska's beautiful Inside Passage with its glaciers and forested islands.

An alternate route from Anchorage is to take the Alaska Railroad from Anchorage to Whittier and from there charter a boat to get into hunting areas of the Sound.

Excellent bear hunting may be had from the middle of May to the first two weeks or so of June, when the bears still have glossy coats. But spring in Alaska arrives erratically, and sportsmen should allow themselves extra days for bad weather. No guide is required by nonresidents hunting black bears, and the current open season of Prince William Sound is September 1 to June 30.

Hunters need a $60 nonresident hunting license, and one $200 tag for each black bear (1987 fee schedule). Flying costs are about $180 an hour for the type of plane we chartered, for about four hours flying time, including pickup, from Anchorage.

Ketch flew in and picked us up the next day.

"In a couple of years you'll see me back up here, maybe for good," B.J. said contemplatively.

CHAPTER XII

DOUBLE ON DEER

Strangely enough, deer fever struck me in the middle of a brown bear stalk on Kodiak Island, Alaska. My hunter, Dick Wanasek, and I were double timing it on a Sitka blacktail deer trail angling up an alder covered mountain. We had just started climbing when I glanced down at the well traveled trail and spotted a shed deer antler. Pausing, I retrieved it and while resting momentarily Dick and I admired it. I placed the antler in my pack and we continued toward the estimated nine-foot bear. Our luck wasn't holding though, and the dark colored bear escaped.

Later, back at our base cabin, I examined the five-point antler by lantern light. The sharply curved main beam was 18 inches long with a circumference between burr and first point of four inches. When spring brown bear hunting ended, a friend and I scored the shed antler by giving it an average spread and matching points. It scored 110 4/8 points, which according to the 1971 edition of Records of Alaska Big Game would have placed it number four in the book.

I decided that as soon as possible I'd return and hunt for the owner of the shed antler. Never having hunted deer, I wasn't sure what my chances would be of finding the buck. After digging up some information, I found that these deer usually inhabit the same drainages they were born in, an area covering a couple of square miles.

I also discovered that our Sitka blacktail deer are considered to be a subspecies of a group which includes the Columbian blacktail and mule deer of western America. The Sitka blacktail is smaller and stockier deer than the Columbian blacktail.

The information didn't help me much at the time, as the fall of 1972, regretfully, slipped by without me being able to alleviate my deer fever.

In the fall of 1973, I was guiding for another outfit. When I finished up the season with them in mid-October, I decided to make the deer hunt and talked my younger brother, Brian, and our father, Denzil, into accompanying me to Kodiak Island.

On November 6, we boarded a commercial airline from Anchorage to the city of Kodiak. Once there, we were delayed for a day when the airlines couldn't find one of our bags. Of course, it had to be the one with Brian's sleeping bag. Luckily, I had brought a double mummy bag and the next day when the airlines still couldn't find the bag, we chartered a Grumman Goose.

It was a relief to reach our mountainous hunting area near Larsen Bay on the northwestern side of the island. Our troubles weren't over though. I had permission to use a 16-foot skiff stored at a nearby cannery and we had just got underway when we discovered a sheared pin on our 7-horsepowered outboard.

We repaired the outboard, and reached our destination a short time later. It was a dilapidated cabin, just large enough for the three of us and our gear, but rain and wind proof to a certain extent.

Since it was early in the afternoon and a calm, sunny day, we set out in the skiff to familiarize ourselves with any sign in the area. We cruised the beach toward the end of the bay and at one point spotted an out of place clump of grass which materialized into a snoozing red fox. On our approach, it nonchalantly stood up and drifted into some nearby brush.

A little later we pulled the skiff up on a gravel beach and shouldered packs and rifles. With the fresh tang of sea air widening our nostrils, we eased around numerous points jutting into the clear sea, hoping to surprise a wayward deer or bear.

At one muddy inlet, we stopped and examined some two or three day old brown bear tracks. My father was hoping to find one of these shaggy bruins and this raised his spirits.

The next morning it was cloudy and 32 degrees when we headed up an unnamed river entering the bay. Near the head of the bay we tied the skiff. The tide was in and we climbed and crawled along a brushy trail to reach the top of some low cliffs overlooking an unwadeable slough. We angled down and crossed the slough at its beginning with our hip boots and started following an old river gravel bed.

It wasn't long before we encountered some fairly fresh deer tracks in a patch of sand. Brian was in the lead. Dad and I wanted him to have the first shot. Reaching the right bank of the river we set off along a worn down combination bear and deer trail. Passing a two-house beaver pond, we slowly hunted our way through some rolling hills at the edge of the river.

Around noon, we stopped near the top of a steep hill overlooking the river canyon to eat sandwiches and canned pudding. We stretched out at the base of a birch tree. Half dozing, I glanced at our rifles and thought most Lower 48 hunters would shake their heads at our choice of deer hunting armament, two Winchester Model 70 .338 magnums and a 7 mm. magnum. But up here you never know when you might stumble upon a brown bear or inadvertently get between a sow with cubs.

When we shouldered our packs again, I drifted into the lead without thinking, since I was familiar with the trail's vagrancies from spring brown bear guiding. To the right of the trail were a series of low ridges with grassy clearings and alder patches dotted here and there with birch, cottonwood and poplar trees. My eyes were continually sweeping the ridge crests in the hopeful expectation that a deer might skyline itself. And then like a shadow from nowhere, a buck was standing skylined about 75 yards away. Its light brown body with white slashed neck was plainly visible, but the antlered head was partly obscured.

Thinking the buck was seconds from bounding off, I swung my rifle up, simultaneously chambering a round, and put the 4X crosshairs on the buck's neck. As my finger tightened on the trigger, I realized the safety was on. I glanced down, flipped it forward and fired. A millisecond elapsed and the buck crumbled in slow motion, with antlers flashing.

We threaded our way through some low alders and fallen birch, and climbed the ridge to find that the buck had dark, heavy antlers with three points on the right side and four on the left. I'd hit him slightly off center in the neck and had to finish him off.

We figured the buck would dress out around 100 pounds, not even close to Alaska's heaviest deer with a recorded dressed weight of 212 pounds. After caping the buck and loading our packs with meat, we headed back for the beach, about a mile and a half away.

In Alaska, 6,000 to 8,000 hunters annually take 10,000 to 15,000 deer and generally prefer still hunting. The hunting season usually runs from August through December with the bucks not quite as wary from mid-October to mid-November as they're in the rut then.

A deer call is used to some extent and is probably about as close to using a stand as Alaskans get, as we don't have the great number of hunters to keep the deer moving. These deer calls will occasionally attract brown bear too, as an employee of Kodiak-Western Airlines found out. Just before we arrived he had called in two brown bears with his deer call, one on each side of him. He wasn't after bear and didn't waste any time in getting out of there.

Some driving for deer is done where the terrain permits it. When winter snows push the deer down to the beaches, they can be more easily hunted but begin losing their antlers the first part of December.

By the time we reached the beach with my deer it was rapidly nearing darkness. We had to drag the skiff for about 100 yards and pole for another 200 before the water was deep enough to start the out-board.

We were cruising along fine when I discovered something black looming out of the water. At first sight, it resembled an island, but I knew there was none on this side of the bay.

"It goes all the way across," Brian gasped in astonishment.

We snaked the skiff across a low-tide created 30-yard wide isthmus. After passing that obstacle, we oared through some seaweed and started off again, only to run into a crab buoy and nearly ensnarled our prop in the line.

Rejuvenated by a good night's sleep, we returned to the river valley and carefully approached the deer carcass, hoping to find bear in the vicinity. A few magpies were on hand to greet us, but no bear or sign of one. The rest of the day was uneventful and after supper that evening we decided that in the morning we'd hunt the valley where I'd found the large shed antler two years earlier.

Before crawling in my sleeping bag, I laughingly told Brian and Dad that I was about due to get a five pointer. Little did I know how this prophesy would turn out!

It was partly cloudy and 26 degrees on November 9 as we took the skiff up to the creek draining Phantom Bear Canyon. This was the name a fellow guide and I had given to a narrow valley where a brown bear had shown up two consecutive springs in the lower alder reaches of the mountains.

We pulled the skiff up past the debris-marked high tide line and climbed a narrow game trial leading over a grassy hill. At the crest, we spread out into a line of sight about 100 yards apart. Numerous small hills and ravines eventually separated us. Dead leaves and grass crunched like a crackling campfire as e, meandered through stands of cottonwood trees, alder brush and pushkin, a hollow reed-like plant that sounds like the crack of a .22 rifle when broken.

Brian was ahead and off to my right somewhere and I thought Dad was back a ways, but he'd unknowingly passed me.

An hour and a half had passed since we started up the valley. I was walking slowly and stopping frequently as I followed a narrow trail dotted with deer droppings along the side of a ridge overlooking a 200-yard wide, willow choked area with a 15-foot wide stream rushing along the outer edge.

Crack! The sudden sound had come from that direction. I fleetingly thought it might be Dad or Brian, but stood there silently and scanned the area.

A huge rack of antlers leaped into my sight as a buck suddenly left his bed. I flipped my rifle up and nearly squeezed off three or four times as he circled in stiff legged bounds toward the main creek. The dense willows effectively screened him from me.

My heart sank when he disappeared into a gully. And when his head cleared it, he was over 100 yards away. He was back in the brush when I quickly glanced ahead and spotted a small grassy clearing in his path. I held the scope cross-hairs about deer shoulder high and squeezed off when I saw the running buck's head.

After the recoil of the .338, I couldn't tell what happened. If he crossed the creek or went down-stream, I might still have a shot. So, I forced myself to wait and watch. When a few minutes had elapsed, I carefully moved down to the clearing. I had searched for a short time and was preparing to circle when I heard Brian whistle. I replied, turned around and discovered the dead buck folded up in some grass about six feet from me. The 250 grain Hornaday had taken him through the base of the neck and nicked the front shoulder.

I happily hollered out, "I got him, Brian." As if he knew what I was talking about.

As Brian came down through the brush I grinned and said,

"A five pointer. "He's got good spread but light bases."

After the 60-day waiting period, Brian and I scored the two sets of antlers several times and had my friend and taxidermist, Tommy Ray, of Anchorage, score them. Our results were very close.

The five pointer scored 98-6/8 -points, having a spread of 14-4/8 inches and longest beam of 14-4/8 inches; the bases, measured between burr and first point, were 4-1/8 inches in circumference. Although with fewer points, my first buck scored 93-1/8 inches with bases of 4-4/8 inches.

Since the 1971 edition of Records of Alaska Big Game requires 90 points for Sitka Blacktail deer, both my deer were eligible for entry. I never thought I'd have the good fortune to double on deer this size, even if the bag limit did allow four deer of either sex. Comparing my deer in the 1971 Alaska record book, I found that the five pointer would rank number 24 out of 35 entries and the smaller one would rank number 33.

That's a better double on deer than any man can expect to find anywhere.

CHAPTER XIII

SIWASH SURVIVAL

"Want to head down and really haul for camp, or stay on the mountain?" I asked, and then warned, "It'll be cold tonight."

Bill Povletich and I were sitting on an eroded rock outcrop overlooking an unnamed glacier valley in Alaska's Wrangell Mountains, after edging along a ledge looking for a full curl Dall ram we had seen. I spotted a ¾ curl and two smaller ones 50 yards below us.

The sun's afternoon warmth was ebbing and if we pushed hard we'd probably make it back to the valley mouth and comfort of our tent and sleeping bags before darkness. But the following morning we'd have to hike back up the narrow valley and repeat a particularly arduous and dangerous climb to regain the altitude needed to reach the full curl ram's territory unobserved.

Bill glanced at his medium weight jacket and extra camouflage shirt. After a brief hesitation he sighed and said,

"Guess I'll stay."

Just over an hour of daylight remained when the air currents finally began angling down mountain so we could descend to a grass-covered slope and glass above us for the ram. The other three sheep had fortunately fed out of sight below us.

Later, in light so bad the ram only appeared as a white blob, Bill shot his first Dall sheep. We gutted the ram by feel and stumbled to the base of an igneous rock outcrop. On hands and knees we scraped out a somewhat level area large enough to allow us to stretch out on.

After we settled down I leaned back and said, "Looks like you'll get to add siwashing to your experience, Bill."

"Siwashing?" he queried, voice still tinged with excitement.

"In Jack London's time siwash was a derogatory name applied to half-breed natives. But today the term is used by many Alaskan sportsmen to mean the spending of an uncomfortable night without the aid of a sleeping bag, tent and occasionally without a fire," I explained.

You can find yourself in a siwashing situation nearly anywhere under a variety of circumstances. I've experienced them on the Alaska Peninsula and Kodiak Island, but usually I'm in Dall sheep and Mountain goat terrain where time is cut short by the distances involved in traveling and back-packing in rough country.

Perhaps you're still-hunting mule deer out West and have decided to return to camp. You suddenly sight a monster buck across a distant canyon, still stalkable before darkness sets in. He's the buck you've seen in your dreams for years but if you try to get him you'll be spending the night without the benefit of your camp.

Then the word hypothermia suddenly materializes in your mind. Your clothing is damp from sweat and your body becomes chilled from a cool breeze as you involuntarily recall some news items of people who died from this dreaded disease.

As most sportsmen are now aware, hypothermia is basically a lowering of the body's inner temperature. Hypothermia is not restricted to high altitude, old or young people, or low temperatures but is usually a combination of getting wet or excessive perspiration, the addition of a cold wind, plus exhaustion and insufficient survival readiness.

Many outdoor articles have dealt with this subject by advising the use of wool clothing and fire as protective measures to combat hypothermia. Sometimes, however, sportsmen can find themselves in an alpine area or in a situation where weather conditions prevent or hamper fire building. In order to effectively counter the effects of hypothermia a heat source outside the body must be utilized to raise the victim's body temperature. This can be done by exchanging wet clothing for dry, insulating the victim from the ground, putting the person in a sleeping bag with another and giving warm fluids (not alcohol which can further reduce the body core temperature) if the victim is conscious.

Because hunters don't normally carry their camp with them as they hunt, they always stand a chance of being caught out overnight and siwashing.

A light survival kit should be carried by every sportsman. The new day and fanny packs are excellent for this purpose and allow a hunter to carry a lunch, small survival kit and rain gear. A hat or stocking cap should also be carried or worn as an uncovered head can lose a vast amount of heat even at temperatures above freezing.

During the past three years I've been carrying a space blanket and some candles as an integral part of my survival equipment. Being an Alaska Master guide, it's my responsibility to have enough survival gear to allow a hunter and myself a reasonable chance of pulling through in an emergency.

The following method I've devised has cured some chattering teeth, warmed some shivering bodies, and enabled me to get some game that might have otherwise eluded me.

I use a standard, large space blanket and stretch it out on the ground, reflective side up. Then I sit down with my legs together, outstretched, so that the blanket is aligned lengthwise with my body, one end just under my knees. The remaining section is pulled up over my back and head and the sides pulled into my body. Two or three clothespins can be strategically placed to hold the sides together, as this method works best when drafts are eliminated and it becomes rather tedious to hold the sides together and keep from moving. A four to six-inch candle sitting on a rock, or more safely in a small cup or empty can, is then placed at ground level between the legs. Space blankets are flammable but require a fair flame and direct contact to ignite. Usually candles go out when knocked over. After lighting the candle the space blanket's two side edges are pulled together in front. With this method, the inside temperature rapidly increases. I used this method in 17-degree weather and found the temperature inside the blanket rose to 55 degrees in five minutes.

The warmest area is around the upper body, and I usually leave a small opening around my face for fresh air when necessary. A space blanket that has been used for a lean-to fire reflector may become smoke coated and pick up a number of small burn holes from campfire sparks which will reduce the overall reflective and heat retaining effectiveness.

The space blanket and candle method is a derivation of an idea used by soldiers in World War I when they used Sterno cans beneath ponchos to warm themselves in the trenches. This technique was predated in principle by the seal oil lamps used by Eskimos.

Ron Kolpin, a hunter from Berlin, Wisconsin, and I had to siwash one night near the end of September in the Alaska Range after taking a caribou halfway up a mountain side. We only had hip boots on for foot gear and had just decided to turn back for our tent camp when I spotted the white maned, heavy beamed 50-inch bull lying below us. Our decision to siwash enabled us to take this fine Barren Ground caribou which could have been out of the area by the time we reached his position the next day.

During the night it rained as we huddled beneath our space blanket. When our chattering teeth and shivering bodies threatened to shake the blanket off, I'd light two candles for about 15 minutes, and we'd be warmed up enough to doze awhile.

The heat produced helped our bodies conserve energy. Shivering also produces heat but at the same time consumes energy and can result in exhaustion. To aid in combating this energy loss I always try to have some chocolate bars along. If heat loss continues, the body's inner temperature will drop. Usually, depending on the individual, shivering is present when body temperature is in the 90 to 99-degree Farenheit range. Thinking becomes impaired from 80 to 90 degrees; unconsciousness occurs in the upper 70's, and death below that.

At the first suggestion of dawn, Ron and I were awake, cold, hungry and tired but in good condition despite the cool temperatures and new snow that had fallen near us. We probably could have survived the night without a space blanket, depending on our degree of wetness, but would have had to exercise considerably.

Before I add something to my back pack it must be fairly light and good for many uses. The equipment for siwash survival, a large space blanket, a few candles and three or four clothespins will only weigh a pound or so and easily meets my guidelines.

Candles are not only useful for siwashing but are excellent for starting fires or for light, while a few clothespins can be handy for hanging wet clothing at camp or used to help start a fire.

The space blanket can be used for siwashing, signaling help, as a rain poncho, ground cloth, or lean-to reflector. Its uses seem to be only limited by the imagination.

Carrying these items as part of your survival equipment may help give you the confidence needed to feel at ease if you must siwash. Siwashing, at best, is not one of my favorite pastimes but when guiding I find myself doing it an average of two or three times a year, usually in the fall but occasionally when brown bear hunting in the spring.

Adding the siwash survival technique to your wilderness lore may be the trick that provides you with a chance for a trophy or gives you life to hunt another day.

CHAPTER XIV

KING OF THE MOUNTAIN

While Dall sheep draw attention like Hollywood starlets, Mountain goats are largely ignored. Sheep venture into near vertical cliffs when necessary to avoid predators, man or animal, but goats seem to enjoy the narrow ledges and sheer rock faces. Apparently they climb them like mountain climbers, "because it's there."

Part of the reason for the low regard goats are held in stems from their small horns and name. Many people equate them to a fancy form of domestic goat while they are actually classified as rupicaprines, or goat antelopes. They are closely related to the chamois of Europe but not to any species in North America.

Hunting our version of the chamois can be difficult or easy, as is the case with most big game hunting. I've had both and some in between.

In the early 1960's goat hunting up Eagle River valley (now a state park) outside of Anchorage was as good as anywhere in

Alaska. The bag limit was two goats and I spent my mountain hunting apprenticeship in those Chugach Mountains.

On one trip I left my hunting companion behind when he balked at climbing a bad cliff face. I made it, barely, and with my Dad's Redfield scoped, pre-64 Winchester .338 slung over my shoulder, continued upward.

Alder patches dotted the cliff tops and I couldn't locate the three goats we had spotted from the bottom. I tried throwing rocks in each likely patch and my third worked.

A billy stepped out 100 yards below me and I quickly laid my rifle over a rock and fired a 250-grain Hornady handload. Red appeared on the goat's shoulder as he toppled out of sight.

Chambering another round I glanced down again and saw a nanny running from the same spot and angling up-mountain. I fired and saw red behind her shoulder but she didn't go down. On my final shot she lurched and fell at the edge of a deep canyon.

I headed toward her and from 50 yards gave her an insurance shot, even though she wasn't moving.

It took considerable coaxing and 50 feet of rope to get my partner up the cliff face.

"That nanny I shot is right there," I turned and pointed as we approached the kill site.

She was gone.

There was a large pool of blood and drag marks where she had somehow pulled and pushed herself over the cliff. It was unbelievable. I carefully crawled to the cliff's overhanging edge and couldn't see the goat in the canyon below.

As it turned out, we would never see her. A small waterfall drained the canyon and despite our efforts we couldn't climb in.

This leads to my first rule of goat hunting: "Never shoot one unless you're nearly 100% sure it will stay where you shoot it."

This is hard to do when you've got a goat dead to rights in your sights but the alternatives are worth considering. You might lose the animal or the meat won't be worth salvaging.

Goat meat, especially from younger goats, is somewhat sinewy but excellent overall if taken prior to the rut. In fact, some people prefer goat over Dall sheep. But if you don't anchor your goat with a good shot the resulting tumbles and bounces off cliffs can ruin the meat as well as horns.

The right rifle caliber can help you get your goat. I recommend something in the .30-06 to .338 range. Smaller calibers such as the .270-7mm calibers work well. I like the added anchoring power of the .30s. Goats aren't large, averaging 150 pounds for billies, but they can reach 300 pounds. Nannies average 125 pounds and can weigh as much as 250. Despite their size, goats can be tough to kill.

Their toughness is vividly expressed by William T. Hornaday, in his 1909 book, "Camp-Fires in the Canadian Rockies." He states: "I once found a big goat, dead, which evidently had been killed by a silver-tip, as there were lots of tracks all around, and the goat's back had been broken. I thought it queer that the bear had not taken the goat away and buried it, as usual, so I looked around. I found a large silver-tip bear, dead, and all bloated up; when I examined him I found that the goat had punched him twice, just back of the heart. He had been able to kill the goat, and then had gone off and died."

The needle sharp headgear of goats are true horns like sheep, and are not shed like antlers. They can be aged by the growth rings and are tougher than many articles state. Still, you might need a pace maker if you watch your trophy topple off a ledge, roll slowly, picking up speed and catapult out of sight over a high cliff.

Speaking of bouncing off cliffs you'd better have the best footgear you can afford. After all, you're competing with the suction-cup-like hooves of mountain goats. Their jet-black hooves are concave on the bottom and give them glue-like holding power on rocky terrain.

I'd recommend a somewhat stiff climbing boot, broken in, but not so much so that the vibram soles are worn, as you're going to need every advantage you can garner. On late September, October and November hunts, crampons strapped to your hiking boots can be lifesavers on partially frozen ground. They're a little cumbersome and you have to be careful where you're stepping in rocky terrain.

Not to scare off prospective goat hunters but you should carry at least 50, preferably 100 feet of 3/8- to ½-inch nylon line or climbing rope. Also, learn to tie a basic bowline, a good non-slipping knot.

This is further reinforced by Joe Back in his book, "Horses, Hitches and Rocky Trails;" he said, "If you give a man enough rope he won't have to hang himself."

My second rule of goat hunting, learned the hard way after being stuck on a cliff face for half an hour, is don't climb a place unless you're fairly sure you can get back down or have another route available. It's easier going up when you can see finger and toe holds.

Hunting in goat country will often put you in some unpleasant siwash situations (in it's extreme meaning - to spend the night without the benefit of fire or shelter), especially on late fall hunts.

On a late November hunt in 1982 at Johnstone Bay near Seward, Ron "Buck" Janson and I spotted a goat on a steep slide above the ocean. Our stalk took us up a near vertical ridge and through large limbed spruce, festooned with hanging moss and occasional swaths of goat hair where they had been rubbing.

We ended up spotting five goats, three on the far side of the slide, and two somewhat closer that had been fighting. One had hair stuck on his horns.

"How big is the best one?" Buck asked as we hunkered behind a mossy spruce stump.

"The billy on the far side is the best, nine or slightly over," I replied. "But he's too far for a good shot and I'm not sure we could get to him."

Judging horn size on goats is somewhat difficult without

experience but some general guidelines are helpful. The length of an adult goat face from horn base to nose is about nine inches. With a bit of imagination you can take the horns off and compare them to the face. A nanny's horns are slender when compared to a billy, who has much heavier bases.

Some, ah hunters, have mistaken ewe sheep and young rams as goats, but adult goats are nearly impossible to mistake. They are blocky in stature, shaggy, both sexes tend to have beards of some sort, and their horns are shaped differently.

Goat hunting is also unpredictable. I remember one hunt several years ago where the wind ruffled the cloud-white hair of the bearded billy as he stood calmly on a narrow ledge, oblivious to the emptiness below him and the hunters nearby.

"There's just no way we can get him," I said to my disappointed hunter.

"Even if we could get closer for a shot there wouldn't be enough to sweep up when he hit the bottom," I added.

"Which one is the biggest of those two on the slide," Buck asked as we watched them slowly feed up the middle of the slide area.

"I'd say the upper one would go about eight inches," I answered.

We waited nearly an hour for the goats to get in a safe spot for a shot. Finally the one we wanted stepped over a log that had been caught on the slide. He was 175 yards away and nearly level with us.

"Now, take him through the front shoulders," I advised.

At the crack of the 30-06 the goat flinched and went down. Buck started to shoot again but the animal lurched to one side and fell out of sight.

Rocks started bouncing down the slide and we stood in silence, waiting for white to appear.

The rolling rocks slowed and quit.

"Maybe he's still there," Buck said hopefully.

We used ropes and crampons to cross the slide, not liking the looks of the pounding surf at bottom. Fortunately, the billy was there, caught in the roots of the tree but in a hole that we had to pull him out of.

Four o'clock darkness, the primary shortcoming of a late fall hunt, caught us just as we got back to the trees. We located a large boulder, one side angled into the ground and the other out of the wind and high enough to let us lean back against it under our space blanket. The first eight hours of siwashing weren't bad. We had some food and would fire up my one burner Coleman occassionally to warm up but by midnight we had about exhausted our conversation.

About then the wind switched 180 degrees, blowing mixed snow and rain into our shelter.

The next sleepless eight hours were miserable, the type best shoved into some dim recess of the mind or relived in front of a crackling fireplace.

Here the trophy was more incidental to surviving the overall trip. We were weathered in Seward for four days (that was an adventure in itself) before getting to camp and it rained and snowed all five days of our hunt.

A trophy goat, like beauty, is in the eyes of the beholder. The eight incher you barely crawled off the mountain with might seem a world record at the time. Serious goat hunters usually consider a goat of nine to nine and a half inches a good one. Goats over nine and a half inches are exceptional and have a good chance of making the "book". The difference between good and "book" isn't much though, which shows why goat horn length is difficult to estimate.

The longest Mountain goat horns on record are listed in the 1981 Boone & Crockett book at 12-4/8" with a base of 4-6/8." Few nannies are listed in the "book", but this one was taken by A. Bryan Williams in the Cassiar Mountains of British Columbia prior to 1916 and is ranked number 212.

The current world record is a magnificent billy that won the Boone & Crockett's prestigious Sagamore Hill Medal in 1949.

Taken by E.C. Hasse in British Columbia's Babine Mountains, this goat scored 56-6/8.

Where can you find your trophy goat?

That's a good question, but you have several trophy producing areas to choose from. "Book" goats have come from the Kenai Peninsula, Southeast Alaska (Chuck Heath took the number 28 goat in 1965 on the mountains overlooking Skagway), Prince William Sound (number 49 was taken near Seward in 1969 by Donald R. Platt, Sr.), Wrangell Mountains, and Chugach Mountains. Kodiak Island is not generally known for goat hunting, but Ron Eller took one there in 1978 that ranks 113 in the "book."

Whether or not your goat makes the record book may be immaterial, but hunting them is mountain adventure in its finest form. Doing it fair chase with respect for the "King of the Mountain" is the mark of a true hunter.

CHAPTER XV

BIG BORE FOR BIG BEAR

Brown bears and grizzlies, now classified by taxonomists as one species, Ursus arctos, have had a history of ferocity, tenacity, and unpredictability since the days of Lewis and Clark. Hunters traveling in bear country today occasionally witness the unbelievable behavior of an adrenalin-charged, brown/grizzly bear.

A large caliber like the .375 H&H or .458 Win. doesn't automatically insure an instant kill. Karl Braendel, a good friend and registered guide, guided Peter Haupt, a Wisconsin hunter, for brown bear on Kodiak Island during the fall season of 1974. Peter was carrying a Ruger Number One .375 and had practiced loading until he was nearly as fast as a bolt-action shooter.

They stalked to within 45 yards of a large bear feeding along a stream for spawning salmon, and Karl cautioned Peter not to fire until the bear was out of the water. The bear abruptly lifted its nose and Karl said, "Get ready!"

Apparently catching a vagrant eddy of man scent, the bear

whirled and headed toward a four foot high gravel bank and the safety of the alders beyond. At the first shot, the bear went down, roaring ferociously, but got back up. Peter's second shot dropped the bear a second time, but it was up quickly, heading for the bank. On the third shot, the bear went down but again made it up and reached the bank. With the fourth shot the bear fell down, but still managed to top the bank and reach the brush where it died.

The 18-year-old, 9-ft. bear had taken four shots, any one of which should have killed him quickly. His adrenalin supercharged body had seemingly rendered him nearly shockproof.

As a hunter and Alaskan guide, I've learned not to be too surprised at the tenacity of the brown/grizzly bear. Judging by this bear, however, a .460 Weatherby would barely be adequate for hunting. General hunting literature often advises potential brown/grizzly bear hunters to shoot the largest caliber they can handle without flinching. This is basically good advice, but a hunter should also be thoroughly familiar with the rifle and be able to shoot it with a fair degree of proficiency. I'd rather have a client able to make a 3" group at 100 yds. with a .30-'06 than a 6" group with a borrowed .375 or .458.

The .338 Win. mag. is my personal choice for hunting brown/grizzly, but my rifle requirements are different than those of the average bear hunter. Rifles such as the .338, .340 Weatherby and .375 are not prerequisites for bear hunting. Neither are the .458 or the .460 Weatherby.

Karl Braendel lost his favorite bear hunting rifle in a riverboat accident several years ago. It was a thumbhole-stocked pre-'64 Winchester Model 70 in .270 Win. with which he had finished off five wounded brown bear and killed one grizzly for himself. I feel the .270 is a little light, without back-up, for brown/grizzly bear, but his bears didn't seem to notice it.

That gun really proved itself on a blustery spring afternoon in 1974. Karl and a Minnesota hunter were stalking a nine foot Kodiak brown bear they'd spotted on a mountain slope mostly covered with alders. Reaching the bear's area, they sighted it in a narrow grassy clearing 100 yards away. The hunter quickly fired his .300 Weatherby Mag. The wounded bear was unaware of their position and ran at an angle toward them through the brush. Karl, unsure of where the bear had been hit, fired his .270 and dropped the bear instantly. The 150-gr. Hornady handload had punched a hole through the bear's skull. The hunter's shot had been good, hitting the heart and lung area, but the bear hadn't seemed aware of it.

In bear hunting one very important factor stands out, second only to marksmanship. When a bear catches a whiff of human scent, hears a dead limb crack, spots unusual movement or is wounded, it immediately becomes more resistant. Putting that first bullet into a bear that is still unaware of your presence is a definite asset.

Such was not the case on a brown bear hunt last year near Uganik Lake, Kodiak Island. I made a heart thudding stalk after an estimated nine foot bear rolling in waist high grass. As I moved in cautiously, the bear frequently raised its head to test the wind. Keeping my .338 nearly raised to my shoulder, I felt my steps out carefully on the snow-patched ground and eased to within 50 yards of the bear.

Then it suddenly sat up and looked directly at me. I still hadn't seen enough of the bear to make a more accurate size estimate, but figuring this was it, I aimed between the shoulders and fired. From a low rise behind me, my brother saw water fly from the bear's right shoulder, but recoil prevented me from seeing the hit. Nearly oblivious to the shock, the bear went down but leaped up and headed for some alders. Working the bolt instinctively I hit the bear again solidly, but it faded into the brush. Quickly, I moved into a narrow clearing paralleling the bear's route. I spotted brown hair at 50 feet, but the bear moved off before I could attempt a shot.

I moved onto the bear's trail, my senses extremely acute because of the danger. Weaving through alders, I broke out into a small stand of cottonwood trees and suddenly spotted the bear 30 yards away near the crest of a low but steep hill. I snapped my rifle up and fired into the bear's shoulder. It reared soundlessly toward me. Much to my amazement, it pivoted and started climbing the hill. Chambering another round, I carefully placed the finishing shot directly between the bear's shoulders. The eight foot bear had been plenty tenacious.

Hunters occasionally drop a bear with their first shot and are reluctant to shoot again for fear of ruining the hide. The veteran guide's advice, "keep shooting as long as they're moving," didn't come about from one hunt; it's based on years of experience.

Non-vital shots happen occasionally when hunting these bears, but they are generally due to difficult shooting rather than poor shooting. Firing at a wounded bear running across ravine-cut terrain or through a stand of alders is not something that can be easily practiced. And brown/grizzly bear along with Mountain goat, are two of North America's toughest species to kill dead in their tracks.

For the first shot on a brown/grizzly standing broadside, I prefer aiming slightly below the shoulder's center, as it allows some latitude for error. A shot farther up or down or back will either break the bear down or kill it.

At the 1974 Alaska Professional Hunter's meeting, a longtime southeast Alaska guide recommended shooting behind the shoulder. This shot is deadly when placed right. But a shot drifted too far back, wounding a brown/grizzly, can necessitate a harrowing, eye-straining, tracking chore.

Getting off such a well placed "text book" shot frequently requires that you catch the bruin unaware. But sometimes the tables are turned. In May, 1973, three of us — myself, Dennis Harms, and Minnesota hunter, G. Schuster — were stalking an estimated nine foot Kodiak bear on a mountain side when Dennis spotted another bear feeding in an alder patch 40 yards below us. Apparently hearing one of us chamber a round, or detecting movement, the bear looked toward us. After the bear dropped its head Dennis whispered, "Better retreat uphill a little."

Watching the alder-screened bear, we stepped back a few feet until our backs were against a line of alders. Then, with no warning, the bear started toward us. The alder tops gently swayed and then began whipping back and forth as it charged. The massive bear broke out into our tiny clearing only 50 feet away. Harms and Schuster fired their .375s nearly simultaneously. I had the gold bead of my .338's front sight centered on the bear's black nostrils but held my fire until needed.

As the two .375s echoed in the valley, the bear tumbled back in the alders. Schuster fired a final shot into the bear's chest and finished it.

Skinning the 9-ft. bear we found that one of the shots had broken the zygamatic arch, the thin rounded band of bone running from the base of the skull to below the eye. This shot likely paralyzed the bear's optical system. One more inch off and the bear might have pressed his charge closer.

These incidents demonstrate that, reasonably speaking, the bore size is less significant than whether or not the bear becomes aware of you and where you place your first shot. A one shot kill with a .270 on an unsuspecting bear is definitely more desirable than seeing a wounded bear escape or having an adrenalin-charged bear collect .338 or .375 slugs like a bullet trap.

Brown/grizzly bear hunters, perhaps more than other North American big game hunters, should be hunters in the true sense of the word. They should be as proficient as possible with their rifles and wait for good shots. There's a big difference between shooters and hunters, and a large bore won't necessarily make-up the difference.

CHAPTER XVI

ALASKA RANGE TRAPLINE

Snowshoe weather had been in effect for two weeks when the ski-outfitted Beaver set us down on an alder-fringed airstrip with a two month supply of grub and 75 traps. It was late November and small flocks of willow ptarmigan had already moved down from the 4,000 foot Alaska Range mountains behind our newly built 12 x 20 foot log cabin, located along a tributary of the Yentna River and 85 miles from the nearest road.

My partner, Karl Braendel, and I were relieving Karl's younger brother, Eric, who had been staying at the cabin and taking care of our seven hunting horses for the past month.

Like many trappers we had often dreamed about running a true wilderness trapline, one free from loose dogs and trap thieves. We were both 26 years old at the time and had resided in Alaska nearly all our lives but our trapping experience had been limited to mink and beaver trapping for the most part close to home.

It was November 24th and the general trapping season had been open for two weeks. Karl and I arrived on the 18th but had been busy cutting wood and hauling horse feed from our mile distant airstrip.

We were itching to string some steel especially since Karl had seen a dark mink in the spring-fed slough 50 yards from our cabin door. This slough meandered into the river about 300 yards from the cabin.

Late in the afternoon of the 24th, unable to restrain myself, I grabbed two No. 1 longsprings and two No. 1 jump traps, slipped my hip boots on, and headed down the slough.

It had that familiar minky look and the sighting of fresh mink tracks set my trapping blood boiling. At the undercut base of a large clump of alders I found one of my favorite spots, a two inch diameter natural hole, eight inches above waterline and with a step-up entrance slickened to ice by traveling mink. The water was about two inches deep at the shore line and I spread a few blades of dead grass over a jump trap to break its' outline, covered the trap chain with mud and fastened the trap wire to a dry stick three feet long and jammed it deep into the mud-bottomed slough.

It was nearly dark when I completed setting the other traps, one bait and two scent sets.

The temperature was a hair above zero in the morning, and before making a feed haul, Karl and I took a quick look at our traps. All were empty. On the way to the airstrip I made some more mink sets while Karl set some marten traps near the mountains.

A plane was supposed to be in to pick up four frozen quarters from a cow moose that Karl had shot on the last day of the season for our parents. When we reached the strip we found that a wolverine had chewed on two of the quarters.

I made a short snowshoe trail about fifteen feet from the moose quarters and made a set similar to a dirt hole set for the wolverine. I put some moose meat scraps and marten scent in the bottom of the hole to simulate a place where a marten had cached some food. Then I anchored the heavy trap wire to our folding sled and covered the No. 3 jump trap with waxed paper and a little snow.

The plane didn't come in so we headed back to the cabin. I decided to check my traps a little closer and had nearly reached the first set when I spotted a mink standing on the bank of a small cove near my set. For a second I wasn't sure that I didn't have a trap there but then the mink moved into the water, it's head out, back barely awash and tail streaming out behind as it swam down the slough.

Around my set the grass had been flattened and the snow battered down. I reached down and grabbed the trap chain leading beneath the bank. At that moment I was feeling disappointed that a mink had escaped, if it was the same one. But to my surprise I felt some strong resistance and pulled out a mink. I quickly rolled the dark male in the snow to clean and dry it. My first mink of the 1974 season would later stretch 31 inches.

November 26th dawned cold and clear and I headed over to the strip with my cross-country skis while Karl later followed with two horses. I checked the rest of our mink sets and crossed the river to our snowshoe trail leading to the airstrip. Seventy-five yards from the strip I spotted some fresh wolverine tracks in the snowshoe trail. My body was tense with anticipation as I followed the tracks toward the strip. Rounding an island of alders I immediately saw the trapped wolverine.

Karl and I had a scale that we used for weighing pack horse panniers during the hunting season and we used it to record the weights of our wolverine. This one was a 22 pound female that later stretched 43 inches. Over the years I had accumulated a number of trapping books but none gave any stretcher dimensions for wolverine, claiming they should be stretched open. That must have been before wolverine became a desirable pelt on the fur market.

I made a two piece stretcher for small to medium wolverine that worked well for us. It was 9¼ inches at the shoulder, 10 and ¾ inches at the base and about 60 inches in length. Karl made a good one for large wolverine that was 10½ inches at the shoulder, 14 inches at the base and about 65 inches in length.

The plane came in later during the day and we received some more horse feed and sent the moose quarters out.

In the morning it was snowing and we checked our traps again, with Karl going upriver while I went down the slough. I had a drowned female mink held by two toes in my blind set and a medium male downriver slightly from where the slough drained in. I pulled my snowshoes out of my pack and went downriver farther to extend my line and made a couple more mink sets and one for a bank beaver.

When I returned, Karl had two marten hanging from the cabin wall. He'd caught one by both front feet in a No. 4 double spring intended for wolverine and the second one in a tree set. We celebrated that night with sourdough bread and moose backstrap.

On the 28th it was raining and we made another feed haul and skinned part of our catch.

The next morning it was foggy along the mountains, temperature in the 30's and still raining. My lucky blind set produced a medium male mink and a beaver had set off my two beaver traps. Apparently I had set them too shallow. I remedied that situation by putting in an alder baited killer trap.

Going farther downriver I encountered another slough, this one strong with the stench of decaying, spawned out salmon. A wolverine had dug out some snow-covered salmon heads but hadn't eaten them. I made two sets for mink and one for wolverine.

Karl had caught another marten and we were satisfied with the way our catch was going. The unusually warm weather had the animals moving and we needed it to make up for our late start.

During the next three days Karl caught one marten and I pulled in a medium beaver from my killer-trap set. Shelf ice had began forming along the river and I had to break through two inches of ice to retrieve the female beaver.

Earl Cook, on left, of Evanston, Wyoming with a 37¼ inch Dall sheep taken at 35 yards with a .270 Weatherby. Zeke on right with Marlin Cook's sheep, a 34 inch ram taken with a 7mm magnum. These rams were taken on the same hunt in a rugged area of the Alaska Range Mountains. Photo by Marlin Cook.

Chris Gutscher of Flint, Michigan with his heavily broomed Dall sheep taken at an estimated 500 yards across a wide canyon with a .270 Weatherby. Ram was 33 inches and taken near the junction of Anderson and Chitina Glacier in the Wrangell Mountains.

Camping on glacial moraine is less than ideal but necessary in order to hunt this rugged country in the Wrangell Mountains where near vertical mountains edge the glaciers. Chris Gutscher of Flint, Michigan wasn't overly impressed with the site. Fellow registered guide, Walt Rowe, is on right.

Zeke, on left, and Pierre Emeric, a Central African professional hunter who resides in Toulon, France, with Dall sheep taken in Alaska Range Mountains. Photo by Don Kann.

Brian (Farley) Schetzle chops out edge of old beaver dam to get Poncho out. It's amazing that he survived the night after falling through the ice.

Deep snow country is hard on horses and man alike on the south side of the Alaska Range Mountains. Horse feed was flown in by bush plane and then backpacked to the cabin.

Young bull moose in caribou country in the Alaska Range during mid-September 1974.

Prince William Sound is a prime area for black bear hunting as well as an area of pristine beauty if one is prepared to endure the rainy climate.

An estimated five foot sow black bear eyed us cautiously as we photographed her.

Bruce Thomas with six-foot black bear taken at six feet with Ruger .44 magnum pistol. Bear taken in Prine William Sound area.

Zeke descends mountain with his Dall sheep. Snow in the high country triples the danger element and any sane person wouldn't be there but sheep hunters are a different breed of hunters.

Zeke took his ram midway up in these cliffs and nearly regretted it when a snowstorm struck and made getting down a more than risky proposition.

Zeke with his 36"x14¼" Dall sheep taken in the Wrangell Mountains on a three day hunt. Hard earned ram could have cost him his life.

Zeke's camp on a glacial moraine left much to be desired but he was so exhausted that he didn't notice the rocks much until morning. The full curl ram was worth it.

Zeke packs out 50 inch antlers and boned out meat of caribou taken by Ron Kolpin on his September 1974 moose/caribou hunt in the Alaska Range Mountains. Photo by Ron Kolpin.

Zeke with "fair chase" Wolverine taken with a Remington .25-06 in the Alaska Range. This was his first wolverine taken with a rifle in many years of hunting and trapping.

Zeke and Kichana Schetzle with the family trapline catch made in six weeks of wilderness living. Author holds the large wolverine pelt. Photo by Glo Schetzle.

John Babler Jr. with his 34½ inch ram taken in the Wrangell Mountains near Chitina Glacier. The steepness of the terrain is readily visible and demonstrates how close we came to losing the ram or having a horn broken or ruining cape and meat. The ram was taken with one shot from John's .300 Weatherby.

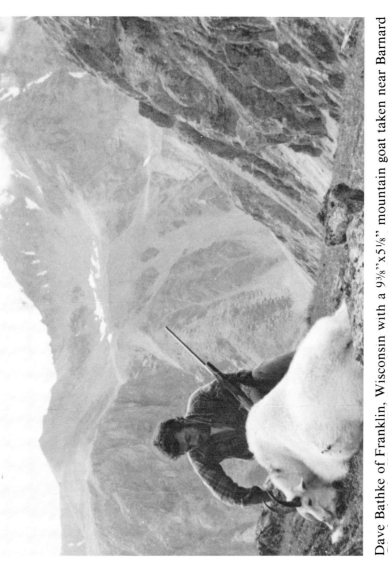

Dave Bathke of Franklin, Wisconsin with a 9⅜"x5⅛" mountain goat taken near Barnard Glacier in the Wrangell Mountains during the fall of 1974.

Author with nine foot Kodiak brown bear taken near Mush Lake, Kodiak Island. Lester Priest of Winfield, Kansas took this nice bear on a spring hunt in 1981. The power of these bears is immense, they could just as easily dislodge your head and a clump of alders. Photo by Lester Priest.

On the third of December I caught a medium male mink in the salmon slough and lost another one along the river. The trap had been wired to a drag but the river had risen during the night and froze the chain down solid about six inches from the trap.

December fifth was cloudy and 24 degrees above zero. I had just crossed the river near the airstrip when I spotted two ptarmigan near some willows. I expended six shots from my .22 pistol and only succeeded in scaring them away. After watching my visions of a ptarmigan dinner fly off I cut over to the mountains and headed upriver setting traps. Karl was working his way up the other side through some heavy stands of spruce trees that provided good marten territory.

I made four marten sets about a quarter of a mile from each other and two wolverine sets. It was dark by the time I returned and found that Karl had picked up another marten in a wolverine set.

The next day I checked my downriver line and caught a light colored marten in a tree set. We found the No. 1½ coil spring to be an ideal marten trap. We made most of our marten sets on extending spruce limbs, about four feet above the ground, breaking off surrounding limbs and securing the trap wire midway out on the main limb. Then we used a short piece of wire to hold the trap in place, but only twisted once so marten would break loose and dangle free once caught in trap. Bait was wired about a foot out from trap and covered with small branches to protect it from birds. These sets are quick and easy to make, and the trap doesn't need to be covered.

December seventh was partly clear and 24 degrees above when I strapped snowshoes on and headed upriver to check my line. The first three marten traps were untouched and between the third and fourth sets I found some fresh marten tracks but they didn't approach my traps.

Then I spotted wolverine tracks coming off the mountain to my snowshoe trail and toward my two sets. I involuntarily quickened my pace. The first wolverine set had been carefully made in my snowshoe trail using a No. 3 and No. 4 double spring. The large wolverine had stepped into the No. 4 and escaped.

My second one, a leaning pole bait set, was around a bend about 15 yards away. Sick and disenchanted from losing the wolverine I shuffled on around the corner trying to figure out what had gone wrong.

I casually glanced at my other set and happily spotted a dark wolverine tangled in a fallen birch.

According to many naturalists the wolverine is a solitary animal except during the breeding season in May, June and July. Karl and I both had experiences where we caught females and found larger wolverine tracks of the same freshness nearby. In these two cases it appeared that a male and female had been traveling close together.

On my upriver line I found that a wolverine would briefly follow or cross my snowshoe trail once every five to seven days.

The female I had just trapped weighed 20 pounds and had a porcupine quill in the face. I caught her beneath a dead birch tree that had fallen against a spruce. After finding a set of wolverine tracks passing beneath the birch I had wired a chunk of moose visera about four feet off the ground and set a No. 3 jump trap and a No. 4 double spring beneath it and two feet apart. As a finishing touch I sprinkled a few meat scraps between the two traps like they had fallen from the bait. The traps were anchored solidly to the spruce tree and covered with wax paper and a skim of snow.

The next day Karl checked his mountain line and I went downriver. Our weather was holding above zero for the most part. Finding some fox tracks I made a blind set and continued checking my line. My last marten set held a large marten and when I reached the cabin Karl had already arrived with another marten and a huge male wolverine. He had caught the nearly black 34 pounder in a cubby set.

Our traps failed to yield anything during the next two days but we were busy skinning and stretching our catch by lantern light anyway. Between the two of us we kept about 50 traps out and about half of these were No. 3s and 4s.

On December 11 Karl caught our first fox in a scent set along a grass-fringed, frozen swamp stream. It was a pale orange female that weighed ten pounds and had two porcupine quills in her nose.

During the night we received two inches of snow and it was snowing as we headed out to check our upriver lines.

It was a nice day for snowshoeing, so quiet you could hear the snowflakes pattering against your back pack. My first set held a large, dark marten with an unusually vivid orange throat patch. The male had been simultaneously caught by a front and rear foot in a No. 1½ coil spring.

The next four marten sets and a wolverine set were empty but when I reached my second wolverine set I could see one of the trap wires stretched out. The set hadn't been disturbed much though. Pulling on the chain I was greeted with a low growl. A nearly black marten, caught by a rear leg, had crawled into a hole and dragged the trap back covering the entrance and giving me quite a surprise.

With two marten in my pack I felt pretty good and headed farther upriver to make another wolverine set.

On my return I barely reached the cabin before dark, since we were down to five and a half hours of daylight, and found that Karl had also picked up two marten.

He had caught one and was on his way back when he discovered some smoking fresh marten tracks heading toward a previously checked set. Following an offshoot of his main snowshoe trail he checked his trap and found nothing. He headed back down the main trail and halted when he suddenly sighted a rapidly moving snowshoe hare. Right behind the hare and hot on it's trail was a marten. The fresh snow was deep enough that at each bound it disappeared when it hit. They went out of sight for a minute and then the frantic hare was coming down Karl's snowshoe trail right at him with the marten still in pursuit. By this time Karl had a .22 long rifle chambered in his rifle.

The hare was so scared that it was within eight feet of Karl before it spotted him. Both marten and hare jumped off the trail and were running broadside when Karl begin following the marten in his sights. When the marten was at the top of a bound Karl squeezed off a shot holding at it's nose. Karl said he really didn't know why he even tried it but at the shot the marten dropped cleanly, hit through the neck at a range of about 50 feet.

In the next eight days we picked up three marten, a mink, and on December 21 it was 10 below when we headed on upper lines again. Passing the airstrip I spooked two moose feeding in a willow patch. Making good time through the deep snow they angled up the base of a nearby ridge and disappeared.

By midday I had reached the last trap on my line and hadn't caught anything. From this trap set I had a good view up the river valley.

Suddenly I caught sight of a moving black object about 300 yards away that was rapidly joined by another one. I crouched on my snowshoes and watched, thinking they were wolverine. But then I saw three more, each jumping a small unfrozen part of the river, their bushy tails flopping as they leaped. The five wolves, four black ones and a tawny colored one, spread out into a line abreast and headed downriver toward me, occasionally dropping out of sight in dips in the terrain.

I pulled my .22 pistol from its' holster and waited breathlessly, knowing my chances of getting a shot were pretty slim even though the slight breeze was in my favor. Prior to this sighting we hadn't seen any wolf sign during our stay or I might have been carrying a rifle.

The wolves continued coming, now in single file, with a large black one leading and the tawny one third in line. Midway across the river was a low windblown ridge of snow that the wolves passed behind. Their backs undulated along the crest, disappearing and reappearing, as they loped by only 75 yards from me. How I wished to have a rifle gripped in my hands. I was tempted to try a shot with my pistol but I harbored wishful thoughts that if I didn't distrub them we might have a chance of one of them blundering into a wolverine set.

They had gone downriver about 100 yards when one of the dark ones stopped and sat down. I eased to my feet and it's ears perked up but it didn't spook. The others were out of sight before this one finally loped off to join them.

Snowflakes were drifting down as I later approached the cabin and the wolves began howling from downriver. It was a low pitched, mournful sounding moaning more than howling, with one wolf occasionally barking.

That was the last we heard or saw of them during our stay.

Karl had also heard them on his way back with a 21 pound female wolverine that he'd caught beneath a slanting birch tree with some bait tucked in the back.

During the next ten days the temperature dropped to a low of 34 below zero but we still managed to catch two more marten.

On New Year's eve we finished off our half-gone supply of medicinal brandy and toasted to a good trapping year in 1975.

After the first we began pulling our traps and by January seventh I had picked up another wolverine, a 20 pound female, and a large male mink.

When our last traps were pulled, wolverine tracks were still plentiful and a marten had been loping along near the cabin.

When Karl's 20 year old brother, Eric, came in to relieve us on January 12 we hated to leave but had to get back to our guiding business.

Our first Alaska Range trapline had hooked us though, and we were already talking about extending our line in the upcoming season.

CHAPTER XVII

ALDER MANIA

The two, young Dall sheep hunters were hunched over, the unpadded straps of their army surplus packboards bearing down unmercifully. Sweat trickled in their eyes and Devil's Club thorns were scattered on their hands and legs like an outbreak of measles. According to local rumor some large rams inhabited the alder protected, high mountain valley they were struggling toward near Eagle River in Alaska's Chugach Mountain Range.

Suddenly the second-in-line hunter, Duane Darby, let out a muffled groan and toppled head first through some twisted alders he had been crawling over. To add to his anger the 60 pound duffle bag tied to his packboard ripped loose and bounced down mountain.

"Stop, stop!" he bellowed, waving his arms as the bag disappeared.

Only those who have been in alder jungles before know this nearly ultimate sense of frustration. I nearly exhausted myself with fits of laughter despite my partner's glaring.

Duane disappeared after the duffel bag and showed up 15 minutes later with the bag wrapped in so much white parachute cord that it would have done credit to an Egyptian mummy wrapper. We didn't get a sheep that trip but it turned into a most memorable alder fight.

Since that time, some 20 years ago, as a hunter and guide I've hunted with numerous companions and have amassed considerable experience in undeclared alder wars in Alaska. As a result, I've gradually been able to classify some of my fellow alder fighters. First though, I'll describe the enemy, who is everything you've heard mumbled about and more.

In the United States and Canada eight species of alder reach tree size but only three are likely to be remembered with deep feeling. These are nicely described in various identification books as sprawling shrubs, hah, occasionally reaching 30 feet tall and six inches in diameter. Their word, "sprawling," is an understatement since these bushes of ill repute grow down mountain, up mountain, laterally, along the ground, intertwined, usually anything but straight. I nearly break into a sweat just thinking about them.

Unfortunately for some of us, the Thinleaf alder (Alnus tenuifolia) a large shrub or tree 15-30 feet high, inhabits much of western Canada, part of the northwestern United States and ranges as far south as the mountains of New Mexico and California. This alder also forms nasty bear inhabited thickets along streams in interior and southcentral Alaska.

The Red alder (Alnus rubra Bong.) occurs along the west coast from California to southeast Alaska. A larger species, ranging from 30-40 feet, this alder is a leading hardwood in the Pacific Northwest. But in southeast Alaska it is of little importance, being more of a nuisance along stream bottoms and land slides where it grows in nearly impenetrable thickets.

Many of my alder skirmishes have been with the Sitka alder (Alnus sinuata), a shrub (not exactly what I call it!) 5-15 feet high or small tree to 30 feet, which is found in Oregon, Washington, western Canada and the lower half of Alaska. This alder often grows in wide belts with alders seemingly as thick as the quills on a porcupine's tail.

These three alders and the American Green alder (Alnus crispa), a sprawling shrub 3-13 feet high which doesn't attain tree size, comprise the four alders found in Alaska. This one has a wide range, occurring in Alaska and also found in Michigan, Oregon and across Canada to Labrador, Newfoundland, and even south to New York and the higher mountains of North Carolina.

Alders are easily recognized, especially when you're whacked by one, by their smooth gray bark with lenticels (horizontal lines) and the clusters of three to nine slender stalked, dark brown conelike fruits generally present. They have irregularly toothed, often shallow lobed, oval to elliptical or oblong leaves, prominently veined.

Hold it now, before you stop reading, remember that one of the tenets of alder warfare is to know your enemy.

The Sitka alder has tear drop shaped leaves, two to five inches long and one and a half to four inches wide while the Thinleaf alder has slightly smaller leaves that are tear drop to oblong shaped.

American green alders have leaves wavy lobed on edges while Red alders have thick leaves with edges curled under slightly and rusty hairs along the veins beneath.

Chances are though, after being surrounded by alders, depending on what type of alder fighter you are, you won't be in any mood to identify the alder that snags your pack, slaps your face or trips you. But with the information listed maybe you'll be able to select a single species to vent your anger on.

I've classified alders fighters into three species and one subspecies. The first one (Alnus silentia), is the silent, determined type, long since out of new swear words, who searches for grassy openings like a professional boxer, or conversely, doesn't look for openings much and just plows through like a moose. Only occasionally does this type, often longtime hunters or guides, show anger. They're just content to escape the alders as soon as possible.

The second species (Alnus muleskinneria), is more common and usually has an unpleasant look on his sweating, red face and swears often with deep feeling. A sub-species (Alnus muleskinneria extria) has the above characteristics but swears louder, engages in futile hand to alder combat, falls often and is occasionally heard mumbling, "What the hell am I doing here, this is supposed to be my vacation?"

The final species (Alnus hystericalia) is an unusual laughing specimen who has an exceptional sense of humor, bordering on hysteria occasionally, and often breaks into mostly good natured swearing, or laughing at the expense of his/her partner. However, this one usually hasn't had many encounters with alders.

To the uninitiated observer, alders may not seem enough to reduce an otherwise normal sportsman (if there is such a thing) to a swearer of muleskinner proportions but regrettably (perhaps, this talent could come in handy for other circumstances) this seems to be the rule rather than the exception. After a hunting trip into an alder infested area your wife or friends may notice some additional flowery expressions in your vocabulary. This is especially true when encountering extenuating circumstances in alders.

They are bad normally but when it rains things become more interesting as they get slimy slick and the limbs under foot treacherous. This will often provide you the opportunity to study alder leaf edges at your convenience when a heavy pack drives you face down into the muck.

The lower Hallet River in the Chugach Mountains is a true hunter's hell (I've often thought if a guide goes to hell it won't be where it's warm but to a never-ending alder patch under perpetual rain). During a rainy fall day in 1974, two Wyoming hunters, one a guide (names withheld to protect the guilty) and I backpacked two sheep from a mountain valley down a typical slope of twisted alders, the wet leaves dripping constantly and cutting off most of the light. These two fellows had only recently been introduced to the debatable pleasures of alder fighting and I could keep track of their progress behind me by the laughter of one and the swearing of the other, depending on who went down. I managed a couple undetected backslides myself and by the time we reached the river we were as wet under our raincoats as if we'd plunged in.

As you perhaps surmise, this alder fighting hunt made a lasting impression on my two companions. For the record, I offered to mail them several alder seedlings for Christmas so they could make Wyoming hunting more sporting by adding some obstacles. They strongly rebuffed my offer and threatened me with bodily harm for making such a suggestion.

Snow adds another dimension to alder fighting and especially during early spring bear hunting. Snags penetrate snowshoe webbing and bowed alder limbs catch you offguard, providing great opportunities for spectacular spills worthy of an Olympic event. Plugged rifle barrels and twanged bows are another aspect of this event.

But for sheer franticness nothing can surpass stumbling into an alder that has a rounded, gray paper-like object clinging to it. A friend, Gabe (Eric Braendel), had such an encounter in the Chugach Mountains and said his feet reacted instinctively to the sight of emerging yellowjackets, only to find that his backpack had snagged up. I imagine he felt like a man going down for the third time just before drowning.

Don Kann, an assistant guide, and I, along with Wyoming hunters, Earl and Marlin Cook, had a similar adventure two years ago in the Alaska Range. We were nearly out to a gravel bar, Don in the lead, when he stopped so abruptly I nearly rear-ended him.

"Bees!" he blurted, turning his head, his eyes rolling like a bogery horse.

As Don turned I glimpsed crawling yellowjackets on a near volleyball size nest, some readying for flight while others were airborne for action. I backpedaled and passed the word to Earl and Marlin. As we scrambled through the thick alders there was a tremendous crash. Don turned to run for it, tripped and fell on his face. Fortunately the bees didn't get him but we sure laughed around the campfire that night, Don not quite as heartily as us though.

Last fall I guided a Frenchman from Africa's Central African Republic for Dall sheep in the Alaska Range Mountains. According to this man before the hunt, the Lord Derby's Eland was the toughest animal in the world to hunt along with the bongo.

After fighting alders on his first Alaskan hunt he changed his mind, "This is toughest hunt I ever go on."

It was generally easy to keep track of him in the alders during the hunt by his sudden outbursts of French.

"What are you saying?" I asked, trying hard not to smile.

"Not very nice things about mothers and god," he grumbled. "You don't want to hear them."

Horses and alders don't mix either, even the horses get mad. You're trying to protect your knees, legs and face when your horse gets fed up and crashes through the brush, hardly responding to your reins, which you don't have a good grip on anyway since you're barely in the saddle by this time. Packhorses also take great delight in testing diamond hitches and pannier construction as they plow through alders. A few years ago, my guiding partner at the time, Giz (Karl Braendel) and I had an independent packhorse named Jughead that rolled in a gully and tangled himself in some alders so badly that we had to chop him out with an axe.

A tall, young fellow named Buck worked with me building a horse trail a few years ago and experienced the raw strength of alders. Using an axe he whacked at an alder a couple of times and it just rolled with the chop. Winding up a super whack he severed the alder and sliced through his engineer boot and into his foot. By the time we reached our cabin his boot filled with blood and he was barely in the saddle. So alders are something to be reckoned with.

Few helpful hints exist for co-existing with and traversing alder terrain. Old watercourses and ravines are often surrounded by alders but occasionally provide an alder free alley up or down mountain. However, this hint might not be as good as it appears since these areas are often occupied by the notorious, broad leafed Devil's Club, which is like grabbing a fistful of tacks should you grab one accidentally.

Going downslope through alders is usually easier than traveling up since you're able to use body momentum to help push the alders away. Removing or lowering the extender bar on a pack can help reduce snagging up.

When moving through alders try to look far ahead and check your side areas for possible grassy openings that will save time and sweat. Don't get so intent on searching for openings that you double your time getting to your destination though. And if you're packing out a caribou or moose rack you may not have much choice.

On hot fall days and long alder slopes, a water bottle or canteen is an asset in reducing temperature and preserving sanity. Above all, stay as calm as possible and don't panic, I've never heard of a man being lost in an alder patch but anything is possible.

Alders aren't totally worthless as they are good for smoking fish and meat. And the Red alder is good for fire place fuel since it reputedly doesn't scatter sparks. Alders in Alaska though, primarily serve as animal cover, a training ground for hunters, and add humus to the ground for more alders.

I must reluctantly admit that on a couple occasions I have been grateful for the presence of alders.

In August, 1971 my brother, Farley (Brian Schetzle), and I made a late afternoon stalk after a ram in the Chugach Mountains and darkness caught us before we reached the sheep. We siwashed with our sleeping bags since the day before a black bear had annihilated our tent and camp. (Fortunately we had been carrying our sleeping bags with our backpacks when the bear incident occurred.)

During the night we slept on a near vertical slope with our arms spread and wrapped around an alder and one jammed between our encased feet. Rain woke us at 4 a.m. and we broke camp. The ram we had been stalking had disappeared, but Farley accounted for a black bear's demise later that morning.

Alders came in handy again during a spring brown bear hunt on Kodiak Island when Wisconsin hunter, Dick Wanasek, and I were forced to siwash in an alder patch. That night we dozed and stoked a meager fire from dead alder limbs. Temperatures slipped into the upper twenties that night and we were grateful for the fire's warmth. However, if the alders hadn't been so blasted thick we might have reached camp before dark.

For my part, I could do without every other alder patch that exists, and in some areas a massive clear-cutting project wouldn't hurt.

If you have managed to survive this chapter it may not be wise to reread it, otherwise alder nightmares might convince you to confine future trips to rabbit hunting on golf greens.

CHAPTER XVIII

BATTERED BUT NOT BEATEN

"You have to be crazy," Doug McRae said, with a shake of his head, "to carry a cannon in your hand and a rifle tied to your pack."

It was strange to carry two rifles, but I was determined to take a Dall ram with a muzzle loader. Doug had helped convince me to pack his scoped Sako 7mm magnum, in case I stumbled across a record class ram unreachable with the blackpowder arm.

My percussion muzzle-loader was an 11-pound .50 caliber. I've owned a .58 caliber Buffalo Hunter and a custom built .54 but this .50 had proven more accurate. My favorite load, 115 grains of Hodgdon FFFg black powder with a 175 grain round ball, had given me my best group, 2-3/16 inches at 75 yards, from a bench rest.

I had managed to obtain four days off from guiding. Guiding is a great occupation but you have to take advantage of any possible chance to hunt for yourself. I was already located in the midst of Alaska's Wrangell Mountains, near the Canadian border.

"Hope you get a 40 incher," Doug hollered shortly before I hiked out of hearing range.

The sun had faded to a dull glow in the sky when I dragged my tired body up a steep, 100-yard-high bluff and set up an overnight spike camp at the base of some rugged saw-tooth mountains.

I forced myself out of my warm mummy bag at 5 a.m. on August 29 and packed without eating breakfast. The drifting morning air was cool enough that I zipped my down vest up as I followed an alder lined game trail toward a nearby glacier valley. By 5:30 a.m. I had reached the valley and started up roller coaster-like piles of glacial moraine. I traveled the valley's right side and used the rock piles as observation posts and cover, in order to slip up the valley unnoticed by any sheep.

From one anonymous rock heap I spotted two sheep barreling down a gravel slide halfway up a nearby mountain. In seconds, I had my spotting scope out of my pack. Just as I focused on them, they reared on their hind legs and slammed heads. They knocked each other shaky, but continued their running game toward the glacier. They were young, half-curl rams, and when I slid back down and continued up valley they immediately sighted me and headed into the rocky crags.

Two hours later I heard the roar of a creek that drained a small, barren glacier valley. Reaching the water, I ate half a package of dried apricots and two candy bars. After drinking enough water to re-hydrate the dried fruit, I refilled my canteen. In glacier country the lack of a canteen can often limit your choice of campsites.

In a few minutes I found a narrow gully and wormed my way up to the top of the creek wall. Slipping my pack off, I settled down and began glassing my side of the valley, quickly noticing two Mountain goats, and then a sheep.

"If it's up there it must be a big one," I thought to myself.

Stretching out behind my pack, I laid the spotting scope

across it. Head up, the golden-curled ram faced up-valley. I was impressed by the heavy bases and wide, flaring horns but couldn't tell anything about the length, other than that he appeared to be a full curl.

From a distance of nearly half a mile, it's difficult to keep things in perspective. A spotting scope compresses the view. Three small valleys may be between you and your quarry, but in the scope it appears as one mountain face. A hunter unacquainted with this effect may be very surprised, and I usually get nailed by it once or twice a year.

Hoping I wasn't due for another one, I checked on the ram and found him in the same position. I slipped on the pack again, picked up my muzzle loader and started the most exciting stalk of my life.

Crouched as low as possible, I scrambled up an open rock slide and angled up valley as fast as I could, hoping to reach a rock outcrop before the ram spotted me. Once there, I noticed the clouds had begun slowly settling below the mountain tops. The wind picked up and some mixed rain and snow swirled into my face.

"Well, at least the direction is right," I thought.

In 15 more minutes, I reached a deeply gouged ravine, in which I again stopped for a rest. I decided to follow the ravine up until I could reach better cover. Trickles of water dripped and streamed down the moss-encrusted rock ledges above me. I recognized the potential danger in this spot, but continued. When climbing, I always plant one foot and check the stability of this footing before lifting my other foot. Now, for the first time in eight years of sheep and goat hunting, I pulled my lower foot up and felt my solid footing slip loose like I'd been standing on butter.

I free fell sideways for about eight feet and crashed down on my left elbow and knee. My muzzle loader flew out of my left hand. I rolled, bounced, and skidded on my side and back for another ten feet or so before I managed to sit up and use my feet and rearend as a brake.

My .50 and I met in the same boulder patch in about the same condition. Its stock was cracked badly in several places and my elbow was bruised severely. My down coat was ripped but had probably helped pad my arm. I held my elbow while I bemoaned the condition of my mangled muzzle loader.

Doug's rifle had only received some minor scratches on the stock and a nick on the scope. The spare glasses in my pack had not fared as well. Sitting on a boulder, I decided I was battered, but not beaten.

I grabbed a fistful of shells, checked the 7mm again, hoping the scope hadn't been jarred out of alignment, and sneaked out of the ravine. I climbed a rocky ridge and found still another separated me from the ram. It now began snowing like winter's first storm.

From that next ridge, I found myself within 600 yards of the ram and couldn't shoot from there. In order to move, I'd have to cross 150 yards of open rock slide, then climb a series of ledges on yet another ridge. Since I had trouble seeing the ram as the wet snow plastered itself on my eye glasses, I figured the ram might be in the same predicament and I moved straight across the slide slowly, stopping frequently.

I climbed a small chute to the top of the new ridge and when I poked my head over at the top, I found another frustrating ridge between me and the ram. This time he was above it.

I didn't think I could approach any closer and decided to shoot. For the first time since I'd spotted him, the ram was feeding broadside. I bellied across some snow-covered grass and crawled down below a rock outcrop on the side of the ridge facing the white ram. I felt my Levi's soaking up the melting snow beneath me and didn't want to lay very long. Pointing the 7mm at the ram, I wiped the scope and my glasses free of snow with some tissue paper. I did this three times before I realized my efforts were being wasted. My down coat had already accumulated a thin layer of snow.

I decided to slide down behind a hummock and circle back to the out-crop so that I could use it to shoot from. Halfway there, a ptarmigan flushed 20 feet away and made a tremendous racket. I froze, knowing I'd been had.

After a short halt to slow my heart, I completed the crawl to the rocks and eased around them so I could see the ram again. Huddled against a rock face I turned my back to the billowing snow and wiped my glasses and scope clean, then glanced at the distant slope again and nearly died from surprise. The ram was gone.

I pulled my binoculars out from under my coat and glassed the mountain side until snow on the lenses obscured my vision. I was in a real sweat.

I stepped out into the open, figuring the ram had moved higher up, and he appeared in plain view like a magician's trick. I dived back into cover. A skift of snow on a large boulder had actually been the ram's exposed back. He was about 250 yards away at a 45-degree angle uphill. I wiped my glass-ware again and rested against the iron-stained outcrop. Holding the crosshairs of the 7mm at the top of the ram's front shoulder I squeezed my shot off.

Whirling, he jumped out of sight in some rocks. I slammed another round in the chamber and stood ready to fire again but the ram failed to materialize. I waited a few minutes and climbed over the intervening ridge. That's when I learned the range was a little more than I had thought. The 7mm had been sighted in to shoot three inches high at a hundred yards, and my shot had been closer to 350 yards than my estimated 250.

Snow was still pelting my face, a half-inch coating the ground, making cliff scaling very dangerous. I wanted to go up after the ram, but if I had any brains I wouldn't.

When I fired, the ram had moved very fast. A sheep usually doesn't react that rapidly, even when shot at, and this one had likely been unaware of me.

So I scaled two tricky rock and grass covered faces and began to have some doubts about being able to return. A 150-foot dropoff doesn't appear very fascinating when snow covers the ground and you're using clumps of grass and rock projections for handholds.

Upon reaching the ram's rock ledges, I angled up to my right and crossed a small, snow-blanketed rock slide. I had the rifle slung over my back as some of the interesting spots required the use of both hands.

A small ledge was becoming visible on my left as I clambered up the slide. When my head cleared the ledge I blinked my eyes in surprise and stood looking at the ram only 100 feet away. He was lying down with his head up and facing into the wind. My first thought was that he was paralyzed or gutshot.

In that second's thought, the ram turned his head, spotted me, jumped to his feet and bounded out of sight. I got a glimpse of his right front leg dangling at the knee.

I jerked the rifle off my shoulder and ran forward desperately. Before I could take two steps the ram appeared between two outcrops above me. In my excitement I cranked a new shell in, forgetting I had put one in earlier. Throwing the rifle to my shoulder, all I saw was snow in the scope. The ghostly white ram had disappeared again.

I just stood there, powerless, and the ram popped into view directly above me on the brink of a sheer cliff about 35 yards up. I swung the rifle like a shotgun and fired. The heavy-horned ram tottered and toppled off the cliff. He fell right at me. It took a very long millisecond for my feet to react, but I got out of the way and the ram dropped directly where I had been standing.

Nightfall was coming on, hastened by the snow-laden clouds. I caped the ram to his head, found the neck joint and severed it with my pocket knife. Then I quartered him and retrieved the backstraps and tenderloins. With the snow situation, I didn't think I could make the trip again so I threw the meat and head off the shortest drop-off I could safely reach.

I began trying to retrace my tracks in the fading light, the 7mm slung. The impressions were barely visible and I had to study the terrain closely to make them out. It was slippery beyond belief when I began my descent. I gulped when my tracks disappeared at the first drop-off.

"Did I come up that?" I marveled.

When I reached the cliff's base, a cool wind whipped my face and I appreciated the chill, glad to be in shape to feel. The snow clouds had finally drifted past me and at that moment I felt like I had when I received my discharge from the Navy.

I hunted for my tracks again and followed them to the edge of another drop-off I had forgotten. When I reached the bottom of this one, my brow was beaded. I made good time on my way back and found my pack at 7:30.

When darkness fell I was on the main glacier moraine and far enough out to be safe from any rock slides. It didn't require much time for me to make a shelter near a granite boulder. Then I scraped out any rocks over two inches or so and rolled my sleeping bag out. After a short meal, my body easily adjusted to the rock bed and I drifted to sleep in minutes.

The harsh cawing of ravens woke me early in the morning. I slipped my glasses on and spotted the ravens lazily circling like buzzards over the area where I had shot my sheep. It had cleared up and was a cool 31 degrees.

I boiled my remaining water for some instant oatmeal and quickly piled my gear to be picked up on the way back.

Ravens are notorious scavengers and with enough company can easily strip a quarter of sheep. I had visions of choice tenderloins and backstraps flying across the valley and this thought provided me with added incentive for speed.

I couldn't see the sheep from camp but as I moved up valley I spotted more ravens circling the area. Shouldering the 7mm I looked through the scope and made out one of the black buzzards standing near a hindquarter. I scrambled up a narrow ravine and climbed until I reached a fractured outcrop.

In a few minutes I discovered the first hindquarter. The remainder of the meat and head were nearby. The Alaska buzzards had made off with one backstrap and shredded a shot-up front quarter. I boned out the other quarters that had landed hide side up.

Before finishing my caping job I measured the ram's horns with a steel tape. They were heavy, 14¼ inches at the bases and 36 inches in length. The ram's wide tip to tip spread of 25½ inches made for an impressive trophy.

It was nearly dark when I made camp short of my spike camp of two nights earlier. I had reached the first growth of alders, though, and scrounged enough dead stuff to build a fire. I prepared a freeze-dried meal and stashed the 7mm close to my sleeping bag in the event a wandering grizzly should stop by for some sheep steak.

Watching the fire flicker I eased my sore elbow down and thought of my hurried hunt. It had been most exciting, but next time I'd put a sling on my muzzle loader and hope for a little nicer weather. I'd hunt exclusively with a muzzle loader and allow myself some additional time so I wouldn't be pressured into any mistakes.

And, as Doug said before I departed base camp, "It's more fun being able to hunt with a friend. Then you have someone to complain to, joke with, and brag to."

Hunting alone is a great adventure, but next time I'd make sure I had a hunting partner in sheep country. Because a fellow could get both battered and beaten, too.

CHAPTER XIX

FAMILY TRAPLINE IN THE ALASKAN WILDS

When the wheel-ski equipped Beaver roared off Anchorage's Lake Hood, my youngest daughter, two-year old Kichana, alias Bop-Bop, peered nervously at the ground. She stiffened and tucked her head between my arm and chest, quivering like a frightened bird.

It was her first plane ride, and I comforted her until she fell asleep.

An hour later the Beaver descended toward our destination, a small unnamed lake near a tributary of the Yentna River in the Alaska Range Mountains. My wife Glo (Gloria) and other daughter, nine-year old Shannon, were packed in with a six-week supply of food, white gas, a chainsaw and trapping supplies.

An uninsulated 10-foot by 14-foot frame cabin was our home for the night of November 14th, until we could snowshoe upriver to a sod-roofed, 12-foot by 20-foot log cabin I used for guiding. It would be our home for the next five weeks or more, depending on weather conditions.

It took us all day to make the two and one-half mile trip to the cabin the next day. Glo was inexperienced with snowshoes and her heavy pack didn't help. I carried Bop-Bop in my pack and alternated pulling a supply-laden toboggan with Shannon.

The cabin was barely discernable in the darkness when we staggered up to it. I fired up a lantern and reassembled the stove pipe, since a bear had apparently knocked it down in the fall. We huddled around the barrel stove until the heat drove us back.

It was five below in the morning and I was itching to "string steel," but we needed more supplies from the lake cabin. I hauled back a larger sled and squeezed in six quick marten sets along the way.

I make all my marten sets as high as I can reach in spruce trees, breaking off any surrounding limbs so marten are forced to travel the remaining branch to reach the scented bait. The spruce limb canopy helps to protect the set from freezing rain and snow, and I cover the bait with small limbs to protect it from birds.

I prefer No. 1½ coilsprings for marten and secure the trap chain to a limb, then use a four- to six-inch piece of baling wire to attach the trap to the limb. However, I only make a half twist in the wire, just enough to hold the trap on. This way the marten is usually hanging dead at the set and doesn't have much chance to break or twist a leg off.

Shannon went with me the next morning and brought us luck. Our fourth set held a beautiful orange-black male marten.

The next day the temperature continued down to 15 below and Shannon and I made another supply run with our packs. We brought back food, white gas, our radio and another, larger male marten that was caught in the same set as the first one.

That night the northern lights were stretched in a broad, shimmering band above the mountains across the river. The nearby spruce trees were silhouetted against the flickering, dancing greenish-white lights, and a gentle breeze brought the muted sound of the river.

"This is where a man should be," I thought to myself as a feeling of peace seeped into my body like the cold.

During the next two days it warmed to two below and I set more traps, this time near the river for wolverine, mink and otter. There was considerable otter sign and I made a two-trap set, putting a piece of wax paper underneath and over the trap pan to keep the traps from freezing up. I had a difficult time keeping the otter set natural, since it was located on a deep river bend with nothing to anchor the traps to. As a last resort I broke a long spruce snag from a nearby swamp and shoved it into the river bottom for an anchor. Judging by past experience, though, the otter probably wouldn't be back. They are mighty suspicious about anything new, even in remote country.

It was a balmy seven above when I snowshoed to the lantern-lit cabin that night.

After a delicious breakfast of steaming sourdough pancakes and canned bacon the next morning, I snowshoed upriver through three inches of new snow that had fallen during the night.

None of my sets had been visited, so I pushed on and found several fresh beaver trails along the river bank. I decided to set a 330 Conibear, but placing the trap was tricky because I had to balance on a narrow ice shelf above the river.

Standing on the bank, I checked the completed set once more and glimpsed a black animal moving down the bank upriver. I thought it was an otter but then saw it clearly on the shelf ice 100 yards upriver.

Wolverine!

It leaped back up the bank and disappeared behind a snow mound. I eased over to my Remington .25-06, chambered a 117-grain Hornady handload and hunkered in the snow, feeling it melting through my jeans.

The dark wolverine was headed toward me, but I only caught a glimpse of it now and then. The suspense of not knowing whether or not it would catch wind of me — plus the cold — kept me shivering.

Suddenly it rounded a mound of snow at the edge of my small clearing and spotted me. I dropped it instantly with one shot at 18 yards.

A non-trapper might not understand the elation I felt then, but anyone should understand the economics of it. Our roundtrip air charter into this area had cost nearly $1,000. This wolverine pelt would later bring $230 and likely be used as parka ruff. In order to stay in the bush country, one has to make a living doing what is available. Even so, at the end of the trapping season I hate to sell my furs. Like most trappers, each pelt brings back vivid memories of a certain day, a good set or a special place.

I stashed the wolverine nearby and continued upriver. Spotting a fresh otter slide, I made a set in the water where one had climbed out and hustled home.

Blue sky appeared the next morning and Shannon and I went downriver. Halfway to the lake we topped a birch-dotted hill and noticed that a wolverine had swung down the mountain and onto our trail.

I picked up our pace, because we had a set nearby. Often when a wolverine gets on your trail it cuts back off after traveling 50 feet or so. This one went to our set, a baited hole beneath a spruce tree, but gone.

"Well, we had one," I said. "But it just snapped the trap."

Thanksgiving morning was twenty above and it was snowing heavily. Six inches had fallen during the night.

"Why don't you take a day off?" Glo asked.

"I better check my upriver traps and get a trail snowshoed in case we get a couple feet," I replied. "But I'll try to get back early."

I worked up a sweat by the time I reached my first otter set. It was buried but I decided to fix it on the way back. My beaver set was kaput. The ice shelf had melted and dropped the trap in the river. I fished the trap out and remade the set.

Even though it was warm I was chilled from sweating, and my parka was soaked from melting snow. I slogged back after making two mink sets — one a blind set and the other a scented pocket set — along a tributary creek. Then I started repairing the sets I'd skipped.

When I approached the first otter set I broke off an alder branch and scraped the snow away from the set. Then, 50 feet ahead, I saw my spruce snag jerk, stop and jerk again, like a fishing rod. A cut bank prevented me from seeing the set, but I assumed the ice had melted and river current was moving the pole.

As I moved forward, fresh otter tracks came into view. I mentally kicked myself for not clearing this set first. Creeping to the edge, I looked into the eyes of a growling otter.

I happily dispatched him and, since it was still snowing, remade the set.

I was beat when I reached the cabin but Glo's holiday meal of ham, fresh baked sourdough bread, potatoes, olives, candied yams and homemade pie helped revive me. There were no after-dinner football games, but I had quite a time skinning and fleshing the otter.

My down-river line failed to produce the next day and I looked forward to heading up-river where the action was.

Two days later I snowshoed up-river again, hoping for better luck since the lake line trip hadn't produced any critters. At my lucky otter set a large mink had swirled on the ice nearby. Further up-river one of my wolverine sets held a marten and along the tributary creek I caught my first mink of the year.

The suspense of trapping, never knowing what you'll catch or if you'll catch anything, is what keeps trappers trapping. Even when fur prices are low, trappers will still be out running their lines. In the remote snow-covered mountains and valleys, you have the freedom of making your own decisions with no one looking over your shoulder, no time clock to punch and no exhaust fumes to breathe. The air is so pure you have to consciously pause now and then to appreciate it.

It snowed two out of the next three days and I spent considerable time resetting traps, but I did manage to catch two more mink and one marten. It was not a large catch, but not bad for a foot trapper.

The second day of December was partly clear and we cut wood until noon. Then I shouldered my pack and hustled up-river, breaking trail through five inches of new snow.

Snowshoeing to my first otter set, I spotted fresh tracks but no signs of a catch. Disappointed, I scraped the snow off my traps. I was down to the ice before I realized the traps weren't there. Mentally scratching my head, I eased over to look in the river. The trap chain led into the darkness.

Putting my rubber gloves on I grabbed the trap wire and pulled. A snapped trap came into view. Suddenly realizing this was the second trap at the set, I tugged harder and pulled out a medium otter.

Farther up-river I flushed a couple ptarmigan, rounded a bend and saw that my Conibear trap was missing. It took me several minutes to untangle and retrieve an estimated 55-pound blanket beaver from the river.

I cached the animals and checked the rest of my line without further success. On the way back I had a bit of excitement, though. One of my snowshoes slipped on an alder branch and the heavy pack drove me up to my armpits at the river's edge.

The next five days I added two mink and an otter to our catch and made two wolverine sets farther upriver. I usually alternate my wolverine sets between cubby sets and hanging bait sets, and use two traps if the terrain allows.

December seventh was windy and 15 degrees when Shannon and I traveled to the lake. We caught a large marten on the way and walked in moonlight for the last half hour home.

The thermometer reading dropped 37 degrees during the night. It was 22 below but Shannon wanted to go with me. Apparently, freezing was preferable to homework. A wolverine had tracked around our last set but didn't go in, so I added more aged moose scraps.

"A weatherman would go crazy here," I thought. The next day, it was partly cloudy and zero.

December 10th was a day that made my journal. Shannon and I checked our up-river line and just before our second otter set, an otter surfaced in the river with a snort of air. It was too risky to try a shot, so we watched it disappear downriver.

At the set, though, a growling otter awaited us. It was an old male, his teeth worn to stubs.

"You brought us luck again, Shannon," I smiled, little knowing how true it was.

We continued on with nothing in our other traps until we reached the last set, visible from a 15-foot high bank along an unfrozen slough. The set area looked like the aftermath of a grenade blast.

"Looks like we had one," I said, muttering curses to myself.

About that time, a mound that I thought was dirt suddenly got up and started growling at us.

We cautiously approached the big wolverine. It's front leg was caught in a 330 Conibear and half of the foot in a 14 jump.

"I don't like this Dad," Shannon said timidly. "I think he's getting loose."

As we watched the angry wolverine chew an inch thick alder in half, she added, "I've got a tree picked out to climb."

"They can climb trees," I said, smiling.

Good swimmers and climbers, wolverines are the largest members of the Mustidae (weasel) family, and can weigh upwards of 50 pounds. I estimated this big male at 40 pounds. That may not seem like much weight, but documented cases describe wolverine killing bull moose (in deep snow), caribou, reindeer and Dall sheep.

That night at the cabin, while skinning, I heard Shannon tell Glo, "I don't want to go again if Dad is going to catch any more wolverine."

The next three days I caught two more marten and a small otter. I helped Shannon make a couple marten sets and she caught our largest male marten. She was so proud of it that she carried it in her arms most of the way. It snowed on two of these days and we received seven more inches of snow. But on December 15th it was raining and 25 degrees. The overflow on the lake was terrible and we worried about being able to fly out of the area on schedule.

I pulled my traps and Glo and I decided to snowshoe a landing strip in a nearby swamp when the rain tapered off. We snowshoed double lines in the wet snow and packed the ends for 100 feet. It was miserable snowshoeing, but we figured if it froze we'd have a fair 1,000-1,200 foot strip.

It cooled the next day and while sitting in the outhouse I heard something heavy approaching. I slowly poked my head out and a moose eyed me curiously from 50 feet away. When it walked by on our snowshoe trail I got the girls so they could watch it.

Later that night I stood alone in front of the cabin, sniffing the wood smoke and staring at the mountains across the river. It was our last night, if the weather held, and this was my personal ritual — a silent good-bye to the wilderness country. It's like being caught between two worlds. You want to leave and you don't. But in the final analysis, you realize that you need both worlds to really appreciate either of them.

Clouds hung below the mountain tops in the morning but the pilot, Dean Carrell, roared in and landed on our strip after circling once. We crawled in, bumped gently into the air and Bop-Bop fell asleep as we left the snowy Alaska Range behind.

Financially, we came close to breaking even on our trapping adventure. But the rewards of bush living brought our family closer and created fond memories that will linger forever.

CHAPTER XX

A GUIDE TO GUIDED HUNTS

Alaska's vast undulating plains of tundra, snow-capped mountain ranges, forested valleys and rain-forest jungles comprise an area that extends 1,100 miles north-south, 2,000 miles east-west and encompasses some of the best wilderness hunting remaining in the world.

Great antlered moose, nomadic caribou, golden-horned Dall sheep, shaggy Mountain goats and massive bears inhabit these areas and are in wide demand by big game hunters around the world.

Contrary to popular belief though, there isn't a wolf or bear behind every tree and outhouse — but enough to keep things interesting.

In order to survive Alaska's climatic conditions, the big game animals either settle into certain mountain ranges, as the sheep or goats do, or travel extensively, as do caribou. Moose and bear do not concentrate much in any one area and are found throughout most of the state.

Locating and judging these animals for hunters is the job of Alaska's 40 master guides, 359 registered guides, 131 Class A assistant guides and 849 assistant guides (these figures accurate as of December 31, 1984). These guide classifications are often confusing to non-resident hunters and require some explanation.

Master guides have been guiding for a minimum of 12 years. They are well experienced and often are booked a year or two in advance.

Registered guides have been guiding for a minimum of three years and may guide for years without getting their master license, since it is not required. The majority of guided hunts in Alaska are booked by registered guides.

Class A assistant guides can do everything a registered guide can do except actually contract for a hunt. These are individuals who have lived and hunted in a particular game unit for many years and are granted this particular license in recognition of that.

Assistant guides must first perform as a packer (during this time they are expected to learn how to cape, judge trophies, survival and other bush craft) for a registered or master guide for a minimum of 30 days and then be recommended for the license. Then they are allowed to work as an assistant guide under the supervision of a registered or master guide.

In order to become a registered guide, an assistant guide must have guided for three years, be recommended by several past hunters, and pass a lengthy written test as well as an oral exam for each of three game units he is allowed to be licensed for.

Assistant guides are the "backbone" of the guiding industry. Without them guided hunts would be tough to find and more expensive, since guides would have to take fewer hunters and charge more. Many assistant guides are content to hold just an assistant license.

This is especially true because Alaska's 26 game units have been divided into exclusive and joint use guiding areas since 1975. These areas were allocated on the basis of usage and investment and divided among the state's master guides and registered guides. Many registered guides do not have areas because they earned their licenses after exclusive areas were allocated or could not prove sufficient usage or investment at the time.

Non-resident hunters who come to Alaska must contract with a master or registered guide in order to hunt Dall sheep or brown/grizzly bear. The exception to this rule is that non-residents may hunt either species with an Alaskan who is within the second degree of kindred to them (mother, father, brother, sister, son or daughter).

Non-resident aliens must have a guide in order to hunt any of Alaska's big game species.

Hiring a guide is unnecessary, though recommended, for residents of other states hunting moose, caribou, black bear, goat, deer and elk in Alaska.

Alaska is such a vast country that many sportsmen feel a guide is necessary to find the game, even though this is not a guide's only function. A guide performs responsibilities rarely realized: cook, photographer, survival specialist, amateur biologist, amateur mountain climber, weatherman, cabin builder, pilot (in many cases), businessman, judging trophies, mechanic, taking care of trophies, part-time psychiatrist (to convince a hunter to climb just one more ridge to get his game), boatman, wrangler, story teller, and, not incidentally, backing you up on big bears.

Three years ago, Michigan hunter Don Fraser and I had a close call with a sow brown/grizzly bear and two cubs in the Shotgun Hills of southwestern Alaska. We were hiking up a narrow, winding tributary creek of a salmon stream when I spotted the three bears walking toward us at a good clip.

The wind was in our faces and they were 80 yards away when I quickly chambered a round in my Winchester .338 and hollered, "Hey Mama, that's about far enough."

She stopped, stood up for a look and charged. By the time I shouldered my rifle she had closed the distance substantially. I quickly fired a round about 15 feet in front of her.

She stopped, slobbering and chomping her jaws. Finally she turned, joined her cubs and disappeared upstream.

Don later said, laughing, "Man, I nearly shot her because I thought you missed."

A complete list of master and registered guides with the areas they are licensed to guide in can be had for $5.00 from the following address:

Department of Commerce & Economic Development
Division of Occupational Licensing
Guide Licensing & Control Board
Pouch D
Juneau, Alaska 99811

The best source of outfitter information and guide business is "word of mouth." If you know someone who has hunted Alaska, buy him or her a dinner and ask questions like a lawyer. This is the best way of getting information.

Booking a guided hunt should be done a year or so in advance to allow a little leeway on a hunt date and to help ensure that you'll get to hunt with your choice of guides.

This is a good time to start getting in reasonable physical shape as well. Sitting behind a desk may be good conditioning for glassing game, but your legs, heart and lungs need to be ready for stalking.

I recommend bicycle riding as a good method of toning your body. If you're going on a sheep hunt it would be wise to carry a pack with 50-60 pounds in it three or four times a week for at least a month to get your shoulders in shape.

Attitude is a little-discussed aspect of guided hunts, but it is important to a happy hunting experience. Being tent bound in a bad storm for a couple days can be a trying experience, but lasting friendships have sprung from such hunts. You can learn more about a person on such a hunting trip than if you knew them for years in civilization.

To help avoid misunderstandings, make sure your guide

knows beforehand exactly what you want in the way of a trophy; a 60-inch moose, eight-foot grizzly or whatever. A guide will do his utmost to give you the best possible estimate of a trophy based on his years of experience.

An old time guide once said, "The only way to really judge a bear is to get close enough to compare it to yourself."

I'm not sure that's the safest way though. After the guide's estimation, it's your final decision to shoot, and that's as it should be.

There are a few hints in contacting and choosing a guide. Don't mimeograph a letter or scribble on a piece of scrap paper and say, "I'm really interested in hunting with you. Send all your information."

Most guides feel that if you aren't interested enough to say what species you want to hunt or even write a letter, then you aren't worth the trouble of a reply and the sending of a four-dollar brochure.

This is an excerpt of a recent, well-written letter requesting information from me:

"I am beginning to investigate outfitters for an archery (possibly rifle) hunt for 1986. I have hunted western states with bow but have some reservations regarding the cost and success for the same in Alaska.

"Not having the time or finances to hunt everything I would like, my greatest interests lie in caribou, Rocky Mountain goat, Sitka deer; black bear and moose are considerations.

"I would greatly appreciate you taking the time to explain your camp, including drop camp costs if you have one; general success archery hunters have; and anything that would help me get a better idea of your hunts."

This was a well-written letter and I always take time to send a good reply for ones like this.

Choosing an outfitter wisely may take some doing as hunts vary widely in length, species hunted, method (horseback, deluxe boat cruise in Southeastern for brown bear, foot, all-terrain vehicles), and cost — from a seven-day, $3,500 spike-camp sheep hunt to $11,000 or more for a 20-day multiple-species hunt. Most hunts fall somewhere between these costs with an average 10-day moose/caribou hunt running around $5,000.

Hunt cost may not be an automatic gauge of hunt quality however. Accommodations vary widely, from minimal tent camps to deluxe lodges. The remoteness of an area and the considerable cost of flying is another variable.

Costs may seem high for hunts and they have gone up considerably over the past decade. The cost of a guided hunt usually includes your air charter in and out with trophies and meat, food, lodging and the services of a guide and packer in some cases.

Don't look for a guaranteed hunt either. Alaska's guide licensing law prohibits such hunts. Besides, anyone who is a real hunter realizes that nothing is guaranteed in hunting, except, perhaps, the enjoyment of being in the wilderness.

After you've narrowed your choice down to three or so guides, it's a good idea to call or write some of the references supplied by the outfitter.

From their feedback you should be able to choose the outfitter you want. At this time I would advise calling the guide, if you haven't yet, just to sort of convince yourself this person to whom you're going to send a deposit really exists.

A deposit of 30 to 50 percent of the actual cost of the hunt usually is required in order to reserve your booking, and may or may not be refundable in the event you can't make it. The outfitter has to hire his seasonal help, buy food and fly in supplies with this money, so if you don't show it's already spent. However, many outfitters will let you send someone in your place or let you come the following year.

Your guide/outfitter will send you an equipment list detailing what you will need for your hunt. This is my suggested equipment list:

- Good quality backpack (not necessary for all hunts)
- Sleeping bag and foam pad or self-inflating mattress

- Hiking boots (well broken in)
- Shoe-pacs (needed for spring or late fall hunts)
- 3 pair of heavy socks and 3 pair of light socks
- Light long underwear
- Several layers of warm clothing (wool & down combinations work well)
- Good quality hip boots
- Gloves
- Rain gear (knee length with hip boots is good or regular raincoat with rain pants)
- Hat (wool stocking cap comes in handy on late hunts)
- Binoculars (spotting scope optional, guide will have one)
- Rifle and two boxes ammo, bow & arrows, muzzleloader & powder/lead
- Light leather slippers/moccasins
- Personal items
- Extra duffel bags for taking meat, capes home

Note: Try to keep your gear to about 75 pounds.

When you arrive at the departure point to fly into camp or at the camp, you will be required to sign a financial renumeration form. This form spells out when your hunt begins and ends, where (what guide area) and who your guide will be.

These forms are also used to prove a guide's use of the area.

One last piece of advice, always check your rifle when you get to camp. And don't be afraid to check later in the hunt if you think you might have bumped the scope. I had a hunter miss a dandy ram because he neglected to tell me he had slipped and rapped his scope.

Good luck and good hunting.

Hunting in Alaska has undergone constant change for more than two decades. Therefore, ALWAYS read current hunting regulations before hunting, or contracting to hunt, in Alaska.